from Journals of the Heart

CARVINGS IN HIS PALM

WHAT GOD THINKS WHEN HE WHISPERS YOUR NAME!

from Journals of the Heart

CARVINGS IN HIS PALM

WHAT GOD THINKS WHEN HE WHISPERS YOUR NAME!

Brenda Craig

Copyright © 2008 Brenda Craig

All rights reserved. This book is protected under the copyright laws of the United States of America. This book may not be copied or reprinted for commercial gain or profit. The use of short quotations or occasional page copying for personal or group study is permitted and encouraged. Permission will be granted upon request. Emphasis and use of Scripture within each devotion, prayer or decree is the author's own.

Scripture quotations taken from the New American Standard Bible®, Copyright © 1960, 1962, 1963, 1968, 1971, 1972, 1973, 1975, 1977, 1995 by The Lockman Foundation. Used by permission. www.Lockman.org)—Scripture quotations taken from the Amplified® Bible, Copyright © 1954, 1958, 1962, 1964, 1965, 1987 by The Lockman Foundation. Used by permission. (www.Lockman.org)—Scripture taken from the HOLY BIBLE, NEW INTERNATIONAL VERSION®. NIV®. Copyright© 1973, 1978, 1984 by International Bible Society. Used by permission of Zondervan. All rights reserved—Scripture quotations marked NLT are taken from the Holy Bible, New Living Translation, copyright 1996, 2004. Used by permission of Tyndale House Publishers, Inc., Wheaton, Illinois 60189. All rights reserved—Scripture taken from the New King James Version. Copyright © 1982 by Thomas Nelson, Inc. Used by permission. All rights reserved—Scripture taken from The Message. Copyright 1993, 1994, 1995, 1996, 2000, 2001, 2002. Used by permission of NavPress Publishing Group.

ISBN 978-1-886296-46-6
For Worldwide Distribution
Printed in the USA
First Printing 2008

Cover Design, Steve Fryer
Editor, Wendy Chorot

Carvings in His Palm, What God Thinks When He Whispers Your Name has chosen to capitalize certain pronouns which refer to Father, Son and Holy Spirit in order to give honor. Our style may differ from some Bible or book publishing etiquette and style. We have also chosen not to capitalize the name satan or any of his related names. In doing this we have given no acknowledgement or prominence to his name or position.

Arrow Publications, Inc.
P.O. Box 10102
Cedar Rapids, IA 52410-0102
319-395-7833
Toll Free: 877-363-6889 (USA only)
Fax: 319-395-7353
www.arrowbookstore.com

Spirit Food for Life Publishing
A Division of Caphar International LLC
P.O. Box 5271
San Antonio, TX 78201
210-663-5067
Fax 830-438-3189
www.journalsoftheheart.com

This book and all other books published by Spirit Food for Life are available:
www.journalsoftheheart.com

Dedication

Carvings in His Palm, What God Thinks When He Whispers Your Name is dedicated to Duane, my husband of 32 years, and my son Daniel. Without Duane there would be no website or book. Without Daniel, my little Prophet who constantly provides me with insight and revelation on a daily basis, many truths shared in this book would not exist. Thank you Duane for all the hours of dedicated work you have invested in this book and the fulfillment of the dreams God has placed in my heart. You are my best friend.

I would like to thank Randall Niles of *www.allaboutgod.com* for believing in me and for being the first one to publish my writings. Without his encouragement, *Journals of the Heart* would not be.

This book is also dedicated to my two close friends, Eustacia Siman Martinez and Veryl Williams and their tireless dedication to the success of Journals of the Heart and to me personally. They provided much inspiration for this book to the glory of God and deserve an immense round of applause. And without the diligent dedication of my editor Wendy Chorot of Inspiration for Writers, who has the ability to edit a prophetic word without changing it, *Carvings In His Palm* would not be the gem it is.

Finally, but not lastly, this book is dedicated to the Lover of my soul, the Lord Jesus Christ and His intimate pursuit of me. It is my desire that His love letters will be a catalyst to a new and passionate relationship of deep communion for all who read this book.

Endorsements

"It is my privilege to be able to recommend this book to all who take the time to dive into its pages. I count it an honor to know Brenda and her family, to serve as their pastor, and appreciate her powerful gifting and revelatory insight beyond what words could express. I am confident that once you've read even just a few pages of this wonderful book, that you will feel a fresh wind of encounter blow into your heart and fan the flames of passion for Christ beyond what you have ever known. I pray that you enjoy and are encouraged by this literary feast and savor every taste."

—William J. Nunez
Senior Pastor
River City House of Prayer, San Antonio, TX

"Journals of the Heart is a must read devotional. Each of the daily devotions will plow deep into the ground of your heart before gently placing God's Word there for daily inspiration. These daily devotions are not only thought provoking, but their impact will linger and mature as the hours pass. Writings such as these can only come from a heart that is deeply devoted and sanctified to God."

—Apostle John Dean
Alliance International Ministries
www.aimteam.org

"It is a delight to write an endorsement for this book. For it contains truths every human being needs to know and apply to his or her life. These are precepts for life; through them we will gain understanding and as the psalmist says "hate every false way" (Psalms 119:104)."

"What you are holding in your hand and reading right now is not an accident. It is not a coincidence. The Lord Himself directed you to this study. This will be the beginning of a new depth of understanding about God and all that He has for you."

"It is my hope that this book will awaken a hunger in all the Father's children for a deeper and richer fellowship with Him. It is my prayer that this clarion call to intimacy with God will touch the heartstrings of every seeking believer. It is my conviction that few will remain the same when they have finished the journey through these pages. May the Holy Spirit, who inspired these words, stir each of us to pursue our own adventure in Him."

—Prophetess Candace House
Author of Shut the Door "It Is Well"
Ruach Chayah Global Ministries, St Marys, GA

What People Are Saying

Journals of the Heart has been an inspiration for me. I have truly enjoyed the writings. When I get to work, reading your journal is the first thing I do. I was raised in a very strict church and have always known God to be vengeful and someone to fear. Through your writings I now know Him in such a new way. I have a new love and passion for my Lord and Savior. Thank you for letting the Lord use you in such a wonderful way. — Benita

Dear Servant of the Most High God, what a special place *Journals of the Heart* is, God's presence is here, I feel His love all in this place…God Bless you and all that you are doing! May your ministry lead many to the light of this world, Jesus Christ and may those that are asleep, find their way to Journals of the Heart and awake from their slumber….I have truly been blessed and thank you for the powerful message that I have received this writing. — Peace & Blessings! Stacy

Three months ago, I came across your website *Journals of the Heart*. I fell in love with the title and the format. At that time I felt I was in the desert. I was looking for something. I know in my heart, it is in God's plan for me that I was led to *www.journalsoftheheart.com*. Since then, everything has been different. From desert to clear springs, from darkness to light, from confusion to hope, and a thousand more changes in my life. To sum up, it is entering into a new season of life; a season of hope, of love, and of restoration. — Tess, Philippines

Dear Brenda, I want to thank you for *Journals of the Heart*. You and this site were a gift from God after my heart wrenching cry to please send me a mentor to help me through this journey of trials. I felt as if I was on a long dusty road all alone, panicking from my own fears. God heard my cries and led me to you, and your site which was like an oasis in the desert for me; a place of rest where the weight of the world has been lifted from my shoulders. My circumstances have not yet changed in the natural, but I have that peace that passes all understanding. Thank you for being faithful to travel your own journey so that God could use you to bring Journals of the Heart to the world. — Veryl, New York

Thank you Brenda, I love your website and I am visiting there more often now! The soaking music is awesome and I appreciate the down loads you have made available. I have very limited finances and every free download is a real blessing to me! Thank you so very much Brenda, and may the Lord bless you with every good and perfect gift as you minister to so many women who are in much need of the love and support you have made available to them (me) through your beautiful ministry and writings! God Bless you my friend! You are truly an awesome woman of God and I appreciate you so very much! — Lots of love In Him, Eva

Hello, this website is so wonderful. It's like the Father. It is actually communicating directly to me. A sister in the lord recommended this wonderful website to me and I thank God she did. I also passed this on to my goddaughter. Thank you so much for this anointed website. I was going to say anointed devotional but it's not even that in my opinion. Like I said earlier, "God speaking directly to you." — Marlene

Contents

Introduction 12
How To Use 14
How To Use in a Group 16

Chapter One - The Gift of Unwavering and Steadfast Faith 19
Long-suffering and Tender-hearted Mercy 26
Contemplation of the Heart 30
Bells of Silence are Ringing 34
Come in all Humility 38
I Am Whispering, Let Go 42
I Whisper, You Emerge, Wisdom Flows 46

Chapter Two - God's Gift of Restoration 51
Precious Time and Shadows of Yesterday 58
Victorious Faith Which Overcomes 62
We Do Things Together 66
I Hear You 70
Dreams, Aspirations and New Wine 74
Your Caring Heart 78

Chapter Three - Walking With Jesus the Good Shepherd 83
I Whisper Sweet Words of Love 90
I Am Your Good Shepherd 94
Free Gifts of Forgiveness 98
Bestowing Gifts of Grace 102
Tears of Beauty and Enduring Grace 106

Chapter Four - The Angels are Dancing..111
    Angel Dance...118
    Such Hope Never Disappoints 122
    Power in the Blood of Jesus 126
    Transforming Love 130
    Your are a Pleasure of My Right Hand.....................................134

Chapter Five - You are a Five Star General in My Kingdom 139
    My Joy is Your Strength..144
    Instrument of Healing and Restoration 148
    Angels of Mercy and Support 152
    Mustard Seed Faith..156
    Arise and Praise Me for I Am Good...160

Chapter Six - Watered Garden of My Love 165
    Garden of My Love 172
    Heed My Call and Be Filled 176
    Three-Stranded Cord...180
    Courageous Heart, Brave Heart...184
    The Favor of Esther...188
    Disengage from Any Entanglement..192

Resources 198

Introduction

Intimately Pursued by a Passionate, Loving God

Carvings In His Palm, What God Thinks When He Whispers Your Name is a prophetic work birthed from the heart of God and whispered into the heart of His beloved. The work consists of a compilation of conversations and dialogs with the heavenly Father as He whispered during the intimate moments of Brenda's life and the lives of her friends, teaching them many overcoming truths. The Word and worship, along with experiences of life, were the catalyst the Father used to teach the truths within as she was inspired by her friends Eustacia Siman Martinez and Veryl Williams, while being intimately pursued by Him.

Each love letter is followed by a *What is God Thinking* journal page. The love letters are then divided into five or six Whispers (devotions) of contemplation which include a prayer of affirmation and declaration, along with questions to reflect and meditate on. A *Whisper Time* has been provided at the end of each Whisper (devotion) to record intimate whispers from the Father's heart to the reader. They can be used in response to the book or the readers own personal life.

The reader is lead on a journey which encourages them to partake of the grace, goodness and mercy of the Lord Jesus Christ. Though written in love letter format, each letter is grounded and based on the Word of God.

Carvings In His Palm, What God Thinks When He Whispers Your Name is designed to present God's point of view in many areas of life, enabling the reader to circumvent destructive pitfalls and receive the encouragement to do it God's way. The underlying theme in this book is God's mercy, grace, and His overwhelming desire to reveal the fact that He sees us in Jesus; with love.

The book's purpose is to teach truth that frees in a loving and personal way and at the same time build an intimate relationship with the Father, removing all fear and creating self-esteem in the reader.

After many years of ministry, marriage counseling, home groups and personal one on one time with God's children, Brenda has come to know intimately the deepest need of a longing heart. *Carvings In His Palm, What God Thinks When He Whispers Your Name* meets this need, creating a sense of oneness with the Father who loves His children and wants them to know it.

These intimate dialogs come directly from the heart of the heavenly Father to the heart of His beloved, enabling a closer communion with Him. Written in this form they become very personal as if the reader is the only one on His mind.

The ultimate goal is to be encouraged to communicate with God on a personal intimate level, opening up an entire new dimension of relationship and receiving from Him.

As a result of reading and participating in reflection and contemplation, the reader will have a growing and increasingly dynamic confidence in the Lord. Come join us as He leads us on the healing journey of a lifetime by speaking His Father's heart into us, His beloved.

How To Use

Carvings in His Palm, What God Thinks When He Whispers Your Name is comprised of six love letters from the Father. Each chapter consists of one complete love letter and five or six Whispers (devotions) derived from said letter. Each Whisper (devotion) is concluded with a time of affirming prayer, reflection and a *Whisper Time* in which to give to and receive from the Father. They are not dated; therefore, have a timeless quality capable of lasting a lifetime.

Begin your intimate time with Father by reading one complete love letter from Him, letting it be absorbed into your spirit. Then take time and respond to the *What is God Thinking* journal page at the end of each letter. Pour your heart out to Him, listen and record what He speaks to you.

We then suggest you read one Whisper (devotion) derived from the complete love letter, daily or at your own pace, in order to ingest and digest, bite by bite, all the Father wants to say to you. Each daily Whisper (devotion) is accompanied by a prayer of affirmation, confession and declaration designed to be prayed and spoken over your life. At the end of each Whisper (devotion) some reflection questions are provided to encourage you to listen and hear what the Father is speaking to you in response to the word through the power and anointing of Holy Spirit. Space is provided to jot down notes to use in future times of reflection.

These questions are meant to be suggestions only. If you are stirred by the questions we provide or by other impressions or thoughts, take the time to respond to them. Start by writing them in your own *Whisper Journal* of love, instruction and remembrance. They become a heritage to your children and a memorial of all God has done and will do (Deuteronomy 29:29). The *Whisper Time* provided at the end of each Whisper (devotion) is meant to encourage you to move beyond prayer and reflection into a place of intimate hearing—into a time of dialoging with the Father.

Remember, the goal is not to hurry through, but instead, get His Word deep into your heart. Therefore, it doesn't matter how long it takes you to get through one Whisper (devotion). Take the time to record all Holy Spirit relays to you. Intimacy and communion is what matters, not time. This is where your own personal *Whisper Journal* will be of great value.

Seize the moment—seize the day, for He is near and ready to whisper to your heart with His words of love.

May the Lord richly bless you and speak into your life. May He make His face to shine upon you. May He bless you in your coming in and your going out. May you hear the whispers of His heart. — Brenda

How To Use in a Group

Carvings in His Palm, What God Thinks When He Whispers Your Name is an excellent tool for small groups. It promotes intimacy with the Father and builds a deep relationship between the members of the group. Consider the example below.

A small group in San Antonio, Texas purchased the book and met together for a six-week period. They began their time by reading a complete love letter together and followed on with a "soaking time or resting in His presence while listening to soothing, worship music" which they downloaded at www.soakingwithapurpose.com. They would then reflect on, discuss, pray for each other needs and journal the whispers Holy Spirit spoke to their hearts. The rest of the week was spent reading the daily Whispers (devotions) related to said love letter. A time of personal soaking followed with reflection and journaling the whispers of Father's heart until they met again. They shared the following testimonies with me.

In Their Own Words

Your Journal – Carvings in His Palm was awesome. After attending your *Soaking with a Purpose Conference* and purchasing a book, a few of us close friends continued the soaking process in order to hear more of what the Lord was speaking to us. In reading one of His letters weekly and using the daily break down as quite time, along with downloading your great soaking music, I cannot began to tell you about the spirit filled time of worship in the presence of the Lord we shared. Your book and music is a benefit to anyone who would want to find calm in the storms of life…Elena

Dearest Brenda…I wanted to share with you the awesome experience I shared with my friends Elena and Rosario after attending your *Soaking with a Purpose Conference*. The effect the soaking session had on our lives that day was so profound that we decided to buy the book *Carvings in His Palm, Jaime Lipe's CD* and schedule a weekly soaking session for the next six weeks. Every Monday we would meet, read the weekly love letter and then follow with a time of soaking. The Lord was so faithful to us; He always showed up and spoke to our hearts. After we soaked we would journal whatever the Holy Spirit laid on our heart. We experienced numerous breakthroughs in our lives. Thank You for sharing this wonderful part of your life with others…Irma

Hi Brenda…I too was so blessed to have shared in this time with Irma and Elena. We met once a week and read a letter from *Carvings in His Palm* and participated in a time of soaking. It was such a blessing to get together in the presence of the Lord and just listen to Him speak to our hearts. Elena would download some of the music found on your website *www.soakingwithapurpose.com* which was a double blessing Thank you…Rosario

Try *Carvings in His Palm, What God Thinks When He Whispers Your Name* in your small group or Bible study and take the journey of a lifetime into a place of revelation and transformation where the whispers of God's heart abound.

Chapter One

The Gift of Unwavering and Steadfast Faith

"Clothe yourselves therefore, as God's own chosen ones (His own picked representatives), [who are] purified and holy and well-beloved [by God Himself, by putting on behavior marked by] tenderhearted pity and mercy, kind feeling, a lowly opinion of yourselves, gentle ways, [and] patience [which is tireless and long-suffering, and has the power to endure whatever comes, with good temper]" (Colossians 3:12 Amplified)

My precious one, My heart is full of loving compassion as I watch you patiently waiting—even if it takes a year or more in your earthly time for your prayers to be answered. Relying on the fact that My words will always come to pass, you wait expectantly and with much anticipation. Full of hope, you strongly believe I am always true to My promises.

You proclaim My promises repeatedly, without tiring. No matter what the situation looks like you hold on to them. Your eyes are lifted up to the heavens, and your steadfast faith never wanes. Your total consciousness is deeply rooted in My Word. In the deep recesses of your soul, My Word has left an indestructible mark. Your whole being contains the stamp of My promises. You savor and relish each one in the silence of your heart. Always hoping, waiting, anticipating and believing, you are My compassionate, faithful one.

While you wait, let tenderhearted mercy always be your companion. It is in long-suffering that your gentleness and kindness of heart have the opportunity to exhibit My nature with incredible joy (Colossians 1:11). In humility and meekness, as you wait for the fulfillment of all I have spoken, make allowances for those who are weaker and without understanding. In this, they will be provoked to trust Me with a heart of love and acceptance. Clothe yourself in Me for you are indeed My compassionate one (Colossians 3:12).

I have dwelt with you in your times of adoration. Your contemplations are sweet, aromatic moments to Me. They waft up through the heavens like sweet perfume and enter My senses like the smell of spring rain. They produce an abundance of fruitfulness in your life as I release them back to you in showers of blessing.

I embrace you in your silence. As you whisper "Shalom," My peace engulfs you (Philippians 4:7). You are lost in Me, apart from the world and transformed into the realm only silence and deep contemplation can make way for. We commune with each other. Our hearts beat in unison, and our minds are entwined within the glory of My loving presence. Such wonderful moments nourish your hungry soul and quench your thirst for My sweet grace. Your heart and mind lifted up to the heights of heaven are enthralled with encompassing joy. Yes, joy and peace transcend your human understanding. A peace that comes from Me, and Me alone, is the garrison of your heart.

These times are important, and you must always remember them. They are like heavenly excursions where I let you taste, touch, and see the essence and beauty of Heaven. Fill yourself when you are with Me, for there will be times you are not in this place of intimate communion. There will be times when cold blasts of stormy weather assault you, making necessary a withdrawal from your heavenly account. An account where you have stored up future nourishment from the joy abiding deep within you at this time—joy bubbling up from deep within your well of salvation (Isaiah 12:3).

Come often to this place of contemplation and silence. Never fear if you feel anxious. It is when you feel anxious or condemned in any way that you should run into this place of shelter and revelation. Take a moment right now, and close your eyes. Take a deep breath, breathing in My presence. I am always here.

The heavens resound with bells chiming through the atmosphere. I have sent angels to ring bells of freedom and jubilation over your life. Clear and precise sounds of purest praise are being sung over your environment as you bow your head in humble submission.

The bells are ringing a clarion call. They release songs, calling My cavalry of angels to arise and come to your aid. Their call is My call to be ready, to clear the ground of your worldly and mundane concerns, for I have come to call it Holy Ground. The quiet contemplations of your worship, the tenderhearted compassions stirred toward others, along with the prayers you have prayed, are arrayed before My throne. You have My attention, and I have yours.

Yes, it is just you and I in an atmosphere of silence—deep silence. A silence so deep you hear even the beating of your own heart as well as Mine (Psalms 131:2). Unmindful of your surroundings or worries, you dwell in My presence. All is well with your soul.

The posture of your heart bowed in reverence and adoration makes the place you abide Holy Ground. In the stillness of the moment, nothing has the power to intrude because it is a moment to moment encounter with Me. I inhabit you, surround you, infuse you, and saturate you to the point of overflowing. Come and spend a few moments with Me right now. All else will wait. I want to touch you deep within, so you can hear the angels ringing the bells of heaven over you right now.

I oppose the proud and give grace to the humble, therefore; I am drawn to you, and My grace abounds (James 4:6). Not only does it abound, but it follows you in sync with its companion, mercy. A humble heart hears, sees what others

The Gift of Unwavering and Steadfast Faith

cannot, and is strengthened by Me (Psalms 10:17; Psalms 113:6).

Your prayerful position is expressive like the sweet kisses a child plants on his mother's face and reminds you to be rooted in the soil of humility. This is truly Holy Ground when you are of such humble attitude and surrender. You yield your total being within the care of My capable hands.

Beloved, bare yourself and hide nothing, ask nothing. Your heart beats out every need you have in sonnets of prayer. In this way, you flow in the Spirit with an abiding faith. How good it feels to forget the world and all concerns that are not heavenly. You must, and will realize, in the end, that only I matter. Keep still, and let Me fill your being. It will be a sight to behold. Oh My beloved, the time has come not to ask or do, but just BE.

I know you have felt the need to perform at times in your life. Others have placed expectations and judgments on you. When you perform at the bequest of others without having a heart of sacrificial love and kindhearted intentions, resentment can form. This robs your quietness in Me, making you feel the need to perform for Me also. All service to others comes out of time with Me or it doesn't bear the fruit of patience, mercy and love. Today I grace you to come always into the quiet place and abide within the very soil of Holy Ground.

As you let go of everything that can come between us in our precious moments of personal encounter, you become all ears to My whispers. My promptings become as vivid and transparent as the clear waters of a mountain spring. Letting go provides a place where you can bathe your whole being in Me, in the loveliness of the moment. You just need to abide.

Always know I plan for your good and not for calamity (Jeremiah 29:11). You have asked for more and more time to be with Me alone, and I am giving it. All you need to do is take advantage moment by moment, and like building with blocks, a beautiful edifice will emerge. Let your heart cry out, "Forever my dear Lord."

I cannot say no to your request for I have seen and felt the humility of your heart, your life. Certainly, I will allow you to be in the deep waters of My love and caring (John15:9; John 16:27). Savor it, feel it, and bathe in the intensity of My powerful and infinite LOVE. Our spiritual union leads you to your destiny. From here, you have a glimpse; I am showing you the vision of all I have planned for you (Jeremiah 33:3). Some things are very clear, others will become clear.

As you leave the Holy Ground of humble adoration and prayer to continue your daily concerns and face new challenges, you receive My anointing. You are stronger to face the realities of life. Should you have to walk in the middle of scorching heat in the fiery path of adversity, you will not be burned. Patience and trust are highly rewarded. Through these experiences, you will have the bread of love and compassion for those going through their own adverse situations. Wisdom born of your own circumstances will feed others and bring life (Proverbs 18:4).

Your creative emergence is blessed by the sweet moments we spend together. Nothing is wasted. I will multiply every aspect of your life. That is My promise. I am opening unusual opportunities and giving you unusual favors. I pour out to you and your loved ones the economy of grace. What seemed difficult and impossible will come to manifest.

I give you the gift of spontaneity in the midst of your creative emergence. I will unlock many hidden potentials the enemy has blinded your eye to. I will blot out doubts, insecurities, and hurts from your memory. There will be complete healing in all areas of your life. I will bring about economic revival and lasting divine prosperity like a river that never goes dry.

I will pour out My blessings to you, and your long-awaited financial breakthrough is happening. I just want to remind you of our covenant. You are just a steward and channel of whatever I will pour into you. I remind you to stay as simple as you are, deeply grounded in My Word. You are to be a living witness for My Kingdom to take over the earth (1 Peter 2:21). Go, my dear precious one. The journey is on.

Prayer

Your words of encouragement have touched my heart beyond measure. It is my greatest desire to fulfill all You have planned for me. Your Word has created pools of refreshing within my being where I can lay and rest when storms of opposition come All I have to do is close my eyes and breathe You in, for the atmosphere around me is filled with Your presence, charged with power, and one-hundred percent available.

You do not run from me and I will not run from you. Many times I get carried away by things going on around me, but today is a different day. I close my eyes and breathe You in once again. Today is a new day—a new day for me.

I give up by faith all tendencies to perform or live up to the expectations of others. If I am in a place of patient humility then all expectations will be met for I will be walking out love. I let go. I acknowledge Your presence and dare to bathe in the essence of Your love. I am captivated, overwhelmed and saturated by You. Your whispers become clear to me in this place of communion with You.

I arise from sitting at Your feet. I arise from the place where my tears wet the ground with praise and adoration. I arise to walk in humble obedience to all I have received—in humble obedience to all You have given. Rivers of life flow from You to me and out of me. I will never grow dry. I am green pastures and still waters to those around me. I journey with You. Amen

Chapter One

What is God Thinking?

Many, O Lord my God, are the wonderful works which You have done, and Your thoughts toward us; no one can compare with You! If I should declare and speak of them, they are too many to be numbered. (Psalm 40:5 Amplified)

Right now The Father is whispering your name and the thoughts of His heart are many, too many to count.

He wishes to pour them over you like sand cascading through a child's hand. Reflect on His tender-hearted mercy toward you and how He has demonstrated it throughout your life.

What is He speaking to you about His steadfastness and faithfulness in relationship to your own personal needs, desires, hopes and dreams?

_____

_____

_____

_____

_____

_____

_____

_____

One

Long-suffering and Tender-hearted Mercy

"Clothe yourselves therefore, as God's own chosen ones (His own picked representatives), [who are] purified and holy and well-beloved [by God Himself, by putting on behavior marked by] tenderhearted pity and mercy, kind feeling, a lowly opinion of yourselves, gentle ways, [and] patience [which is tireless and long-suffering, and has the power to endure whatever comes, with good temper]" (Colossians 3:12 Amplified)

My precious one, My heart is full of loving compassion as I watch you patiently waiting—even if it takes a year or more in your earthly time—for your prayers to be answered. Relying on the fact that My words will always come to pass, you wait expectantly and with much anticipation. Full of hope, you strongly believe I am always true to My promises.

You proclaim My promises repeatedly, without tiring. No matter what the situation looks like, you hold onto them. Your eyes are lifted up to the heavens, and your steadfast faith never wanes. Your total consciousness is deeply rooted in My Word. In the deep recesses of your soul, My Word has left an indestructible mark. Your whole being contains the stamp of My promises. You savor and relish each one in the silence of your heart. Always hoping, waiting, anticipating and believing, you are My compassionate, faithful one.

Chapter One

While you wait, let tenderhearted mercy always be your companion. It is in long-suffering that your gentleness and kindness of heart have the opportunity to exhibit My nature with incredible joy (Colossians 1:11). In humility and meekness, make allowances for those who are weaker and without understanding. In this, they will be provoked to trust Me with a heart of love and acceptance. Clothe yourself in Me for you are indeed My compassionate one (Colossians 3:12).

Waiting on a Whisper

Affirmation

Lord, Your words of encouragement have touched my heart beyond measure. It is my greatest desire to fulfill all You have planned for me. Your Word has created pools of refreshing life within my being where I can lay and rest when storms or opposition comes.

When I ponder Your love and patience for me, my patience grows for those around me. I am a dispenser of Your tender heart with kindness, gentleness and a good temper. Patience and long-suffering are my opportunities to walk in a way truly representing Your heart of humility. Thank you. Amen

Reflection

What have you been waiting patiently for? How has your attitude or faith level been?

Read the devotional scriptures and, cloak yourself with the words by putting your name in them. Proclaim them over yourself and you will see change.

Chapter One

Whisper Time

It's whisper time…Time to breathe Him in…Time to listen and reflect on what He has spoken to you and respond to the Waiting on a Whisper reflection questions or your own thoughts and insights. He is present…He is speaking your name… What is He saying?

Begin your own dialog with the Lover of your soul and journal your very own whispers to and from His heart, even if it is only a few words. Remember, He is always whispering and He is waiting for you to listen to His heart. He has awesome words of love and instruction to convey to you today.

_____

_____

_____

_____

_____

_____

_____

_____

_____

_____

Contemplation of the Heart

"And God's peace [shall be yours, that tranquil state of a soul assured of its salvation through Christ, and so fearing nothing from God and being content with its earthly lot of whatever sort that is, that peace] which transcends all understanding shall garrison and mount guard over your hearts and minds in Christ Jesus" (Philippians 4:7 Amplified)

I have dwelt with you in your times of adoration. Your contemplations are sweet, aromatic moments to Me. They waft up through the heavens like sweet perfume and enter My senses like the smell of spring rain. They produce an abundance of fruitfulness in your life as I release them back to you in showers of blessing.

I embrace you in your silence. As you whisper "Shalom," My peace engulfs you (Philippians 4:7). You are lost in Me, apart from the world and transformed into the realm only silence and deep contemplation can make way for. We commune with each other. Our hearts beat in unison, and our minds are entwined within the glory of My loving presence.

Such wonderful moments nourish your hungry soul and quench your thirst for My sweet grace. Your heart and mind lifted up to the heights of heaven are enthralled with encompassing joy. Yes, joy and peace transcend your human understanding. A peace that comes from Me, and Me alone, is the garrison of your heart.

These times are important, and you must always remember them. They are like heavenly excursions where I let you taste, touch, and see the essence and beauty of Heaven. Fill yourself when you are with Me, for there will be times you are not in this place of intimate communion. There will be times when cold blasts of stormy weather assault you, making necessary a withdrawal from your heavenly account. An account where you have stored up future nourishment from the joy abiding deep within you at this time—joy bubbling up from deep within your well of salvation (Isaiah 12:3).

Come often to this place of contemplation and silence. Never fear if you feel anxious. It is when you feel anxious or condemned in any way that you should run into this place of shelter and revelation. Take a moment right now and close your eyes. Take a deep breath, breathing in My presence. I am always here.

Waiting on a Whisper

Affirmation

I have often embraced my times with You and heaven has seemed to fill my heart to the point of bursting. I often wonder when things are hectic and stormy how can I possibly forget the moments in Your tangible presence. But I do so many times.

I will choose to walk according to Your Word and not let any dullness or anxiousness of heart keep me from You. All I have to do is close my eyes and breathe You in, for the atmosphere around me is filled with Your presence, charged with power, and one-hundred percent available. You do not run from me and I will not run from You. Amen

Reflection

Reflect on some of your more intense moments with Him while your heart was given over to complete adoration. Even if they were brief, they have the capacity to change your life. Draw on them. Let them become a catalyst to move back into His presence.

Chapter One

Whisper Time

It's whisper time…Time to breathe Him in…Time to listen and reflect on what He has spoken to you and respond to the Waiting on a Whisper reflection questions or your own thoughts and insights. He is present…He is speaking your name… What is He saying?

Begin your own dialog with the Lover of your soul and journal your very own whispers to and from His heart, even if it is only a few words. Remember, He is always whispering and He is waiting for you to listen to His heart. He has awesome words of love and instruction to convey to you today.

_____

_____

_____

_____

_____

_____

_____

_____

_____

_____

Bells of Silence are Ringing

"Surely I have calmed and quieted my soul; like a weaned child with his mother, like a weaned child is my soul within me [ceased from fretting]" (Psalms 131:2 Amplified)

The heavens resound with bells chiming through the atmosphere. I have sent angels to ring bells of freedom and jubilation over your life. Clear and precise sounds of purest praise are being sung over your environment as you bow your head in humble submission.

The bells are ringing a clarion call. They release songs, calling My cavalry of angels to arise and come to your aid. Their call is My call to be ready, to clear the ground of your worldly and mundane concerns, for I have come to call it Holy Ground. The quiet contemplations of your worship, the tenderhearted compassions stirred toward others, along with the prayers you have prayed, are arrayed before My throne. You have My attention, and I have yours.

Yes, it is just you and I in an atmosphere of silence—deep silence. A silence so deep you hear even the beating of your own heart as well as Mine (Psalms 131:2). Unmindful of your surroundings or worries, you dwell in My presence. All is well with your soul.

The posture of your heart bowed in reverence and adoration makes the place you abide Holy Ground. In the stillness of the moment, nothing has the power to intrude because it is a moment to moment encounter with Me. I inhabit you, surround you, infuse you, and saturate you to the point of overflowing. Come and spend a few moments with Me right now. All else will wait. I want to touch you deep within, so you can hear the angels ringing the bells of heaven over you right now.

Waiting on a Whisper

Affirmation

Many times I get carried away by things going on around me, but today is a different day. I close my eyes and breathe You in once again. I can never do it enough. All of eternity will not be adequate time to experience You. I have often felt like my moments with You haven't been plentiful enough to get Your attention, but they have. You value each and every moment I spend with You. Help me see the grandness of it all, and cause me to hunger and thirst after You with every fiber of my being. I am here. Touch me and let the bells ring. Amen

Reflection

Have you been too busy to close your eyes for even a moment or felt if all you have is a moment it isn't enough, so you decline? Remember, minutes, hours, days and weeks are built in increments. Enough minutes and you have a day, a year.

Close your eyes for a moment; whisper His name and imagine the clear sound of church bells ringing. What is He saying? What are His bells ringing in your heart?

Chapter One

Whisper Time

It's whisper time…Time to breathe Him in…Time to listen and reflect on what He has spoken to you and respond to the Waiting on a Whisper reflection questions or your own thoughts and insights. He is present…He is speaking your name… What is He saying?

Begin your own dialog with the Lover of your soul and journal your very own whispers to and from His heart, even if it is only a few words. Remember, He is always whispering and He is waiting for you to listen to His heart. He has awesome words of love and instruction to convey to you today.

_____

_____

_____

_____

_____

_____

_____

_____

_____

_____

Come in all Humility

"O Lord, You have heard the desire and the longing of the humble and oppressed; You will prepare and strengthen and direct their hearts, You will cause Your ear to hear" (Psalms 10:17 Amplified)

"Who humbles Himself to behold the things that are in the heavens and in the earth" (Psalms 113:6 NKJV)

I oppose the proud and give grace to the humble, therefore; I am drawn to you, and My grace abounds (James 4:6). Not only does it abound, but it follows you in sync with its companion, mercy. A humble heart hears, sees what others cannot, and is strengthened by Me (Psalms 10:17; Psalms 113:6).

Your prayerful position is expressive like the sweet kisses a child plants on his mother's face and reminds you to be rooted in the soil of humility. This is truly Holy Ground when you are of such humble attitude and surrender. You yield your total being within the care of My capable hands.

Beloved, bare yourself and hide nothing, ask nothing. Your heart beats out every need you have in sonnets of prayer. In this way, you flow in the Spirit with an abiding faith. How good it feels to forget the world and all concerns that are not heavenly. You must, and will realize in the end, that only I matter. Keep still, and let Me fill your being. It will be a sight to behold. Oh My beloved, the time has come not to ask or do, but just BE.

I know you have felt the need to perform at times in your life. Others have placed expectations and judgments on you. When you perform at the bequest of others, without having a heart of sacrificial love and kindhearted intentions, resentment can form. This robs your quietness in Me, making you feel the need to perform for Me also. All service to others comes out of time with Me or it doesn't bear the fruit of patience, mercy and love. Today I grace you to come always into the quiet place and abide within the very soil of Holy Ground.

Waiting on a Whisper

Affirmation

I receive Your grace and mercy today and I allow it to shape my life and actions toward myself and others. I bow in humble adoration within the secret place, letting my silence be like the kisses of a child. May the beating sonnet of my heart touch Your heart, creating an abiding flow of Holy Spirit in my life.

I give up by faith all tendencies to perform or live up to the expectations of others. If I am in a place of patient humility, all expectations will be met for I will be walking out love. I move from doing to being…I can feel Your breath blowing the cob-webs of the past away as my humility creates a place, a sanctuary, even Holy Ground. My time has come to BE. Amen

Reflection

Reflect on the thought of your heart beating out a sonnet of prayer when you are in a place of humble adoration. There are not enough words or expressions available to describe the sonnet of your heart. It is a heavenly language and He hears.

Chapter One

Whisper Time

It's whisper time…Time to breathe Him in…Time to listen and reflect on what He has spoken to you and respond to the Waiting on a Whisper reflection questions or your own thoughts and insights. He is present…He is speaking your name… What is He saying?

Begin your own dialog with the Lover of your soul and journal your very own whispers to and from His heart, even if it is only a few words. Remember, He is always whispering and He is waiting for you to listen to His heart. He has awesome words of love and instruction to convey to you today.

_____

_____

_____

_____

_____

_____

_____

_____

_____

_____

_____

I Am Whispering, Let Go

"My soul yearns, yes, even pines and is homesick for the courts of the Lord; my heart and my flesh cry out and sing for joy to the living God" (Psalms 84:2 Amplified)

"As the Father has loved me, so have I loved you. Now remain in my love" (John 15:9 NIV)

"…No, the Father himself loves you because you have loved me and have believed that I came from God" (John 16:27 Amplified)

As you let go of everything that can come between us in our precious moments of personal encounter, you become all ears to My whispers. My promptings become as vivid and transparent as the clear waters of a mountain spring. Letting go provides a place where you can bathe your whole being in Me, in the loveliness of the moment. You just need to abide.

Always know I plan for your good and not for calamity (Jeremiah 29:11). You have asked for more and more time to be with Me alone, and I am giving it. All you need to do is take advantage moment by moment, and like building with blocks, a beautiful edifice will emerge. Let your heart cry out, "Forever, my dear Lord."

Chapter One

I cannot say no to your request for I have seen and felt the humility of your heart, your life. Certainly, I will allow you to be in the deep waters of My love and caring (John15:9; John 16:27). Savor it, feel it, and bathe in the intensity of My powerful and infinite LOVE. Our spiritual union leads you to your destiny. From here, you have a glimpse; I am showing you the vision of all I have planned for you (Jeremiah 33:3). Some things are very clear, others will become clear.

Waiting on a Whisper

Affirmation

I give You everything…everything…everything. Yes, I give You everything, from the greatest need to the smallest. I give You all wrong thoughts about our relationship. You are not far from me. On the contraire, You are very near for You live within me. I am Your abiding place—Your home in this earth. I let go. I acknowledge Your presence and dare to bathe in the essence of Your love.

I am captivated, overwhelmed and saturated by You. Your whispers become clear to me. The eyes of my understanding are open to wisdom and revelation. My moments with You are arising into an edifice of praise and communion. Help me to continue in this place of abiding love. Never let me stray from Your hand of comfort and protection. You abide in me and I in You. Yes, I abide. Amen

Reflection

What things always seem to get in the way when you pull aside to spend intimate time with Him? Look for a pattern of having the same old issue or doubts appear to discourage you, lie to you, thereby disrupting the flow of communication with Him.

In the natural, bathing is cleansing and enjoyable at the same time. The bathing process takes place to wash away and invigorate. With this in mind, take some time to bathe in a place of worship and let His sweet whispers forgive, cleanse and fill up all in the same process. What freedom this is. Reflect and write what He tells you to do in order to maintain this freedom and cleansing.

Chapter One

Whisper Time

It's whisper time...Time to breathe Him in...Time to listen and reflect on what He has spoken to you and respond to the Waiting on a Whisper reflection questions or your own thoughts and insights. He is present...He is speaking your name... What is He saying?

Begin your own dialog with the Lover of your soul and journal your very own whispers to and from His heart, even if it is only a few words. Remember, He is always whispering and He is waiting for you to listen to His heart. He has awesome words of love and instruction to convey to you today.

_____

_____

_____

_____

_____

_____

_____

_____

_____

_____

I Whisper, You Emerge, Wisdom Flows

"The words of a [discreet and wise] man's mouth are like deep waters [plenteous and difficult to fathom], and the fountain of skillful and Godly wisdom is like a gushing stream [sparkling, fresh, pure, and life-giving]" (Proverbs 18:4 Amplified)

As you leave the Holy Ground of humble adoration and prayer to continue your daily concerns and face new challenges, you receive My anointing. You are stronger to face the realities of life. Should you have to walk in the middle of scorching heat in the fiery path of adversity, you will not be burned.

Patience and trust are highly rewarded. Through these experiences, you will have the bread of love and compassion for those going through their own adverse situations. Wisdom born of your own circumstances will feed others and bring life (Proverbs 18:4).

Your creative emergence is blessed by the sweet moments we spend together. Nothing is wasted. I will multiply every aspect of your life. That is My promise. I am opening unusual opportunities and giving you unusual favors. I pour out to you and your loved ones the economy of grace. What seemed difficult and impossible will come to manifest.

I give you the gift of spontaneity in the midst of your creative emergence. I will unlock many hidden potentials the enemy has blinded your eye to. I will blot out doubts, insecurities, and hurts from your memory. There will be complete healing in all areas of your life. I will bring about economic revival and lasting divine prosperity like a river that never goes dry.

I will pour out My blessings to you, and your long-awaited financial breakthrough is happening. I just want to remind you of our covenant. You are just a steward and channel of whatever I will pour into you. I remind you to stay as simple as you are, deeply grounded in My Word. You are to be a living witness for My Kingdom to take over the earth (1 Peter 2:21). Go, my dear precious one. The journey is on.

The Gift of Unwavering and Steadfast Faith

Waiting on a Whisper

Affirmation

I arise from sitting at Your feet. I arise from the place where my tears wet the ground around Your feet. I arise to walk in humble obedience to all I have received, in humble obedience to all You have given. I have drawn my strength from You. I receive grace for myself and I stand on behalf of my family to receive much mercy and grace.

Every area of my life will respond to Your healing touch, even to the deepest subconscious thoughts and memories. I relinquish them all, seen and unseen, known and unknown, by faith. My life will flow forth within Your economy and not according to what I see. I am Your living witness and I emerge in to fullness. Rivers of life flow from You to me and out of me. I will never grow dry. I am green pastures and still waters to those around me. I journey with You. Amen

Reflection

Reflect on the specific words of declaration He has made in this devotion and confess anything necessary to bring new life. Respond in agreement and walk out the wisdom He has already given to you. There is always someone who knows less about certain things than you do. Ask Father to lead you to His hungry, needy sons and daughters.

Chapter One

Whisper Time

It's whisper time…Time to breathe Him in…Time to listen and reflect on what He has spoken to you and respond to the Waiting on a Whisper reflection questions or your own thoughts and insights. He is present…He is speaking your name… What is He saying?

Begin your own dialog with the Lover of your soul and journal your very own whispers to and from His heart, even if it is only a few words. Remember, He is always whispering and He is waiting for you to listen to His heart. He has awesome words of love and instruction to convey to you today.

_____

_____

_____

_____

_____

_____

_____

_____

Chapter Two

God's Gift of Restoration

"Until the day breaks and the shadows flee away, [in my thoughts] I will get to the mountain of myrrh and the hill of frankincense [to Him whom my soul adores]" (Song of Songs 4:6 Amplified)

My dear precious one, you have been so quiet for such a while. I see many changes in you. I am thrilled at the transformation going on. There is no wasted time in Me, and you have set your priorities right. Your time is spent more on contemplation, and you are engrossed in your duties to the things I have called you to—like home, work and family. This is good.

How pleased I am at how your heart and all you do is focused on Me. I am pleased by your awareness of how everything is connected with Me. My love for you is manifesting in many ways; the heavens declare the glory of it. Oh yes, My dear precious one, it is beyond any shadow of doubt that nothing—yes, nothing—can separate us (Romans 8:37-39). How tender your love is for Me! I rejoice in it.

Yet, I see little traces of anxiety in your heart. I know the cares, the condemnations, and the trials of the past you have been through. I looked down from heaven and witnessed your every struggle. My unseen caring hands strengthened you. Your hopeful heart is always lifted up to Heaven, waiting for My readiness to come to your side whenever you face trouble. I am your ever-present help in time of trouble (Psalms 46:1). Trust Me, and let's move on to higher ground, to the hill of frankincense (Song of Songs 4:6).

You believe beyond your human understanding in all My restoring graces. How can I ever say no to your pleadings when you have so much hope in My goodness? Your anxieties are only shadows of yesterday. It is time to let them go. Be anxious for nothing, Beloved (Philippians 4:6). I care for the sparrow, and I care even more for you (Luke 12:6-8). Relax in the security of My love today. Do not worry about tomorrow, and the shadows will flee.

Your faith is like the faith of a little child. You look not on what is around you but on My promises. My heart bleeds afresh with tender mercy whenever I see your misty eyes. I wipe your tears with gentle breaths of wind, sweeping them to Heaven where I collect them. I pour them back over your life with a gentle rain of promise and answered prayer. They are incense to Me. Please, in all you do, remember, love covers a multitude of sins—yours and those around you.

To wake you, I warm your heart with the morning sunshine. I serenade you with a song each time your heart sings a note of love to Me. I love your smile whenever you are delighted with the tiny blooms you see sprouting up everywhere along the way. I make manifest My loving presence in My creations, showing you how much I love you. Today is your day, My child, your day to experience the essence of My great love for you. Open yourself to the immense possibilities of immeasurable love. You have victorious, overcoming faith. This faith conquers the world (1 John 5:4-5). Yes, this faith conquers all fear and doubt. Restoring graces fall like sweet spring rain. Turn your face upward, and let your heart become a deep reservoir of precious treasure. Look up; I am here.

You are never alone in the wee hours of the day or any other moment in your life. I have always been there, even when you weren't aware. We do things together, you and Me. You are one who declares My works (Psalms 73:28). Your touching words of spoken endearment are enabled by inspiration of Holy Spirit. I sit beside you whenever you pour your heart of love out to Me. Just the movement of your lips saying My name warms My heart and makes Me smile. Ah…what beauty you are.

I embrace you tight whenever you are afraid. I comfort you whenever you feel lonely. I make you aware of My presence every time a little bird sings among the gardens I have placed around you. Many times when you hear a bird sing, he is singing over you, rejoicing over the garden you are to Me. Do you not notice how bright the solitary star of your life shines? I don't think you do, and I am here to show you because I want you to see and know you are My "Shining Star." I touch you, just to say, "Beloved, I am here with ravished eyes of love. You are at the center of My gaze."

I show My tender touch whenever someone who loves you, kisses you. I confirm My love for you whenever you are embraced in arms of love. Like a sweet child embracing his mother, I am overjoyed and moved to draw near. When My promptings excite you the same way as the sweet giggles of a child thrill the heart of a mother, I rush in to give you more. Yes, when you draw near, I draw near (James 4:8).

I hear your voice each time you recite your favorite scripture, your favorite Psalm. You always say, "The Lord is my shepherd, I shall not want" (Psalms 23:1). Your proclamation is confirmed whenever I deliver your needs and answer your prayers for the people you love so much. You will never be wanting for more because I have given you a contented heart. All you need to do is receive it and say, "I have a contented heart." Confess this often when storms appear on the horizon to threaten you in any way or lusts of the flesh entice you.

Any vain desire for the most refined and beautiful things can be satisfied by seeing Me in all My fullness. Seeing and touching the finer things of life can create an appreciation for the unlimited talents distributed among My created ones. Never feel others have more creative ability when you see the expressed talents of their lives. Share a moment of joy and rejoice, but never compare yourself. Someone else is looking at you, marveling at your gifting and creativity. Let little moments of joy capture your heart. Beloved, let Me touch the sorrows of your heart for I am your JOY.

I hear your every word, your every syllable, yes, even the sound of your breath as you inhale and exhale (Psalms 10:17). I prepare your heart and cause you to hear Me as well. Continue to call on Me, knowing beyond a shadow of doubt, I hear you. I hear you before a sound is ever formulated (Psalms 17:6). I listen in advance, in preparation to act. Come boldly!

Your dreams are no secret to Me. Do not be ashamed to have big dreams. Am I not your BIG GOD? I am proud of you whenever you speak My words of wisdom. Oh, My beloved, you are coming to terms with life. You are becoming sure of yourself in Me. I am happy with your newly acquired self-confidence. You are emerging, yet you remain humble and always rely on the graces from above. I will be very pleased if you remain docile and gentle. A gentle and quiet spirit I do not despise. I am a God of restoration, and I am restoring. Have faith.

The meek inherit the earth, and those who hunger and thirst after righteousness are satisfied (Matthew 5:6). Open your mouth and I will fill it with a new hunger beyond your highest longing (Psalms 81:10). The awakening of your heart makes it seem as if you could explode with the grandeur of it all. Yet, there is so much more.

You see, I take your old wine skin and make it new. You were made a new creature at salvation, and now I am regenerating what I have given you in order to hold more (2 Corinthians 5:17). New wine is coming, and you must be ready (Matthew 9:17).

Close your eyes for just a moment. Can you see Me? Can you hear Me? I am near. My breath is brushing across you. Embrace the moment. Embrace Me. I love seeing your intense concern for the well-being of others (Galatians 5:14). Your compassion and generosity are the very reasons why I cannot and will not withhold My blessings.

I know you will be My channel of grace. I have made you to be so. If there is any contradiction to this in your life, choose to believe Me, not the circumstance. I trust in the covenant you made with Me to be a person dedicated to the well-being of others. In this, you fulfill the two commandments to love Me and your neighbor as yourself.

I read your thoughts, and I know you profoundly. I know your struggles to erase the dark spots of yesterday that endeavor to hinder your growth. Do not worry if there are challenges. This is the way of life. I was challenged and depended on every word proceeding from the Father (Matthew 4:4). So must you, depend on every word Holy Spirit speaks to you.

Are we not walking together, journeying on the path we agreed to (Amos 3:3)? The path I chose before all time. I will walk with you all the way, never leaving or forsaking you. I will take you by My BIG HAND. I will be your shield against all enemies and your light in the dark, enabling you to encounter Me, to encounter My voice—the still small voice whispering to you the right words to say, the right way to go (Isaiah 30:21).

Yes, we encounter each other, and My hand leads you to the path we agreed for you to tread…I will always be with you, My beloved one. There is no other place I would rather be. All is restored in Me, regenerating what I have given you in order to hold more. You are a new creature (2 Corinthians 5:17). New wine is coming, and you must be ready. I am.

Prayer

Lord, all my time belongs to You. There is no other more worthy than You. Thank you for taking my times of contemplation and quietness and multiplying them for Kingdom purposes. I refuse to give into worry or fear. I surrender the little anxieties of my heart.

You, who formed the worlds and hold them together by Your great power, can take care of my small world, even to the minutest detail in the lives of those I love. Teach me to trust without fear, for You are faithful even when I am faithless.

You are my ever-present help. Most of all, You are my all consuming passion. I give myself wholly to You. I receive Your regenerating move of love in my life and my wine skin is being made new. New wine is flowing into my heart and mind. I am renewed in You. I am a new creature made to display manifestations of Your glory in the earth. All is made perfect in Your loving care. Amen

What is God Thinking?

Many, O Lord my God, are the wonderful works which You have done, and Your thoughts toward us; no one can compare with You! If I should declare and speak of them, they are too many to be numbered. (Psalm 40:5 Amplified)

Right now The Father is whispering your name and the thoughts of His heart are many, too many to count.

He wishes to pour them over you like the waters of a trickling stream. Reflect on His ability to overcome the shadowy places of your life and impart to you a victorious, overcoming faith. He hears you, so tell Him about all the things in your life in need of restoration and listen.

Write down any personal revelations. These are your weapons of warfare for yourself and those you love.

_____

_____

_____

_____

_____

_____

_____

_____

_____

Precious Time and Shadows of Yesterday

"Until the day breaks and the shadows flee away, [in my thoughts] I will get to the mountain of myrrh and the hill of frankincense [to Him whom my soul adores]" (Song of Songs 4:6 Amplified)

My dear precious one, you have been so quiet for such a while. I see many changes in you. I am thrilled at the transformation going on. There is no wasted time in Me, and you have set your priorities right. Your time is spent more on contemplation, and you are engrossed in your duties to the things I have called you to—like home, work and family. This is good.

How pleased I am at how your heart and all you do is focused on Me. I am pleased by your awareness of how everything is connected with Me. My love for you is manifesting in many ways; the heavens declare the glory of it. Oh yes, My dear precious one, it is beyond any shadow of doubt that nothing—yes, nothing—can separate us (Romans 8:37-39). How tender your love is for Me! I rejoice in it.

Yet, I see little traces of anxiety in your heart. I know the cares, the condemnations, and the trials of the past you have been through. I looked down from heaven and witnessed your every struggle. My unseen caring hands strengthened you. Your hopeful heart is always lifted up to Heaven, waiting for

My readiness to come to your side whenever you face trouble. I am your ever-present help in time of trouble (Psalms 46:1). Trust Me, and let's move on to higher ground, to the hill of frankincense (Song of Songs 4:6).

Waiting on a Whisper

Affirmation

Father, my heart is fixed on You and as I look around I see the manifestation of Your glory. I am loved with a tender love. Every struggle I walk through is in Your hands and I am saved from my enemies; worry, doubt, unbelief and fear. I trust in You Lord. All my tomorrows are in Your hands and Your precious blood separates my sin from me as far apart as east is from west. I walk in overcoming faith and I am embraced within Your loving care for You contend on my behalf.

Your Word is always on my lips and in my heart. Every sound of prayer, worship and adoration, even to my slightest breath or sigh of praise is heard and treasured by You. Even my thoughts of love toward You reach the highest heavens with angelic grace. Today my heart is enlarged to hold more of You as new wine is poured into the recesses of my spirit. I hear Your voice and follow You on the covenanted journey we have agreed upon. Amen

Reflection

Did you ever stop to contemplate how much the Lord is pleased with you? Now would be a good time.

What little anxieties have you let into the peaceful manifestations of His heart in your life?

Take some time to let His declaration of love and constant attention seep into your heart.

Chapter Two

Whisper Time

It's whisper time…Time to breathe Him in…Time to listen and reflect on what He has spoken to you and respond to the Waiting on a Whisper reflection questions or your own thoughts and insights. He is present…He is speaking your name… What is He saying?

Begin your own dialog with the Lover of your soul and journal your very own whispers to and from His heart, even if it is only a few words. Remember, He is always whispering and He is waiting for you to listen to His heart. He has awesome words of love and instruction to convey to you today.

_____

_____

_____

_____

_____

_____

_____

_____

_____

_____

Victorious Faith Which Overcomes

"For the [true] love of God is this: that we do His commands [keep His ordinances and are mindful of His precepts and teaching]. And these orders of His are not irksome (burdensome, oppressive, or grievous). For whatever is born of God is victorious over the world; and this is the victory that conquers the world, even our faith. "Who is it that is victorious over [that conquers] the world but he who believes that Jesus is the Son of God [who adheres to, trusts in, and relies on that fact]?" (1 John 5:3-5 Amplified)

You believe beyond your human understanding in all My restoring graces. How can I ever say no to your pleadings when you have so much hope in My goodness? Your anxieties are only shadows of yesterday. It is time to let them go. Be anxious for nothing, Beloved (Philippians 4:6). I care for the sparrow, and I care even more for you (Luke 12:6-8). Relax in the security of My love today. Do not worry about tomorrow, and the shadows will flee.

Your faith is like the faith of a little child. You look not on what is around you but on My promises. My heart bleeds afresh with tender mercy whenever I see your misty eyes. I wipe your tears with gentle breaths of wind, sweeping them to Heaven where I collect them. I pour them back over your life with a gentle rain of promise and answered prayer. They are incense to Me. Please, in all you do, remember, love covers a multitude of sins—yours and those around you.

To wake you, I warm your heart with the morning sunshine. I serenade you with a song each time your heart sings a note of love to Me. I love your smile whenever you are delighted with the tiny blooms you see sprouting up everywhere along the way. I make manifest My loving presence in My creations, showing you how much I love you.

Today is your day, My child, your day to experience the essence of My great love for you. Open yourself to the immense possibilities of immeasurable love. You have victorious, overcoming faith. This faith conquers the world (1 John 5:3-5). Yes, this faith conquers all fear and doubt. Restoring graces fall like sweet spring rain. Turn your face upward, and let your heart become a deep reservoir of precious treasure. Look up; I am here.

Waiting on a Whisper

Affirmation

Lord, You are so attentive to my prayers and You hear me before my lips have a chance to speak. I am more than a sparrow to You. I am the love of Your life. Your creation shouts words of love to me. Help me to notice the depth of Your beauty and be content in You.

I have a heart of child like faith and You honor me. My heart is a rejoicing heart full of abundant praise. You have displayed so much beauty before me. Your love covers me and Your blood bought the forgiveness of my sins. I lift up my heart to the Lover of my soul. Rain is falling on my upturned face. I am Your reservoir of unlimited love. Amen

Reflection

Are there areas in which your heart needs to be warmed with the Son-shine of His love? Write them down, relax in posture of praise and let Him sing over you.

Record what He says and speak it over yourself.

Since His ears are attentive to your prayers, what do you want to ask of Him? Have the faith of a child, knowing He loves you and ask.

Chapter Two

Whisper Time

It's whisper time…Time to breathe Him in…Time to listen and reflect on what He has spoken to you and respond to the Waiting on a Whisper reflection questions or your own thoughts and insights. He is present…He is speaking your name… What is He saying?

Begin your own dialog with the Lover of your soul and journal your very own whispers to and from His heart, even if it is only a few words. Remember, He is always whispering and He is waiting for you to listen to His heart. He has awesome words of love and instruction to convey to you today.

_____

_____

_____

_____

_____

_____

_____

_____

_____

We Do Things Together

"But it is good for me to draw near to God; I have put my trust in the Lord God and made Him my refuge, that I may tell of all Your works" (Psalms 73:28 Amplified)

"Draw near to God and He will draw near to you" (James 4:8a NASB)

You are never alone in the wee hours of the day or any other moment in your life. I have always been there, even when you weren't aware. We do things together, you and Me. You are one who declares My works (Psalms 73:28). Your touching words of spoken endearment are enabled by inspiration of Holy Spirit. I sit beside you whenever you pour your heart of love out to Me. Just the movement of your lips saying My name warms My heart and makes Me smile. Ah…what beauty you are.

I embrace you tight whenever you are afraid. I comfort you whenever you feel lonely. I make you aware of My presence every time a little bird sings among the gardens I have placed around you. Many times when you hear a bird sing, he is singing over you, rejoicing over the garden you are to Me. Do you not notice how bright the solitary star of your life shines? I don't think you do, and I am here to show you because I want you to see and know you are My "Shining Star." I touch you, just to say, "Beloved, I am here with ravished eyes of love. You are at the center of My gaze."

I show My tender touch whenever someone who loves you, kisses you. I confirm My love for you whenever you are embraced in arms of love. Like a sweet child embracing his mother, I am overjoyed and moved to draw near. When My promptings excite you the same way as the sweet giggles of a child thrill the heart of a mother, I rush in to give you more. Yes, when you draw near, I draw near (James 4:8a).

Waiting on a Whisper

Affirmation

I am never alone and I cling to Your promises in the Word. You never leave or forsake me. I am always on Your mind. Your wings encompass me in the secret place when I am afraid. Help me to see how I shine for You on days I can't see the Son.

Kiss my life with Your grace and mercy. Let my heart flow forth with goodness and all right thinking. Like a child, I draw near to You, embrace You, cling to You and confirm my love with a heart of thanksgiving. I giggle like an excited and delightful child in Your presence. Fill me to overflowing as I rejoice with songs of praise. Amen

Reflection

Are there areas in your life in which you are afraid? What are they? Tell Him. He already knows. He wants to embrace you in your places of fear.

Take some time to be—to be in His presence and let His love penetrate the circumstances of your life. Listen for His song.

Chapter Two

Whisper Time

It's whisper time...Time to breathe Him in...Time to listen and reflect on what He has spoken to you and respond to the Waiting on a Whisper reflection questions or your own thoughts and insights. He is present...He is speaking your name... What is He saying?

Begin your own dialog with the Lover of your soul and journal your very own whispers to and from His heart, even if it is only a few words. Remember, He is always whispering and He is waiting for you to listen to His heart. He has awesome words of love and instruction to convey to you today.

_____

_____

_____

_____

_____

_____

_____

_____

_____

_____

I Hear You

"I have called upon You, for You will hear me, O God; Incline Your ear to me, and hear my speech" (Psalms 17:6 NKJV)

"LORD, You have heard the desire of the humble; You will prepare their heart; You will cause Your ear to hear" (Psalms 10:17 NKJV)

    I hear your voice each time you recite your favorite scripture, your favorite Psalm. You always say, "The Lord is my shepherd, I shall not want" (Psalms 23:1). Your proclamation is confirmed whenever I deliver your needs and answer your prayers for the people you love so much. You will never be wanting for more because I have given you a contented heart. All you need to do is receive it and say, "I have a contented heart." Confess this often when storms appear on the horizon to threaten you in any way or lusts of the flesh entice you.

    Any vain desire for the most refined and beautiful things can be satisfied by seeing Me in all My fullness. Seeing and touching the finer things of life can create an appreciation for the unlimited talents distributed among My created ones. Never feel others have more creative ability when you see the expressed talents of their lives. Share a moment of joy and rejoice, but never compare yourself. Someone else is looking at you, marveling at your gifting and creativity. Let little moments of joy capture your heart.

Beloved, let Me touch the sorrows of your heart for I am your JOY.

I hear your every word, your every syllable, yes, even the sound of your breath as you inhale and exhale (Psalms 10:17). I prepare your heart and cause you to hear Me as well. Continue to call on Me, knowing beyond a shadow of doubt, I hear you. I hear you before a sound is ever formulated (Psalms 17:6). I listen in advance, in preparation to act. Come boldly!

Waiting on a Whisper

Affirmation

You are my Good Shepherd and provide all my needs. Sometimes I don't understand why things are the way they are, but I trust You. Let my heart always be content in every circumstance. Storms may arise and many things may entice me, but You will be my one love—my one desire.

I will not compare myself to others. I embrace who You have made me to be. I will draw from the gifting of others and give in return. I surrender every sorrow and embrace Your radiant beauty. I draw deeply from the wells of salvation and receive Your heart of joy. All I will ever need is found in You. Amen

Reflection

Have you compared yourself with someone else and come up short in your own eyes? Confess and agree with who He says you are; His beloved favorite one.

Surrender your sorrows for they rob joy. Drink from the fountain of gratefulness and speak with a voice of thanksgiving for all He sacrificed for you. Joy will come and invade your heart.

Record your joyous thoughts and use them as weapons against the assaults of the enemy.

Chapter Two

Whisper Time

It's whisper time…Time to breathe Him in…Time to listen and reflect on what He has spoken to you and respond to the Waiting on a Whisper reflection questions or your own thoughts and insights. He is present…He is speaking your name… What is He saying?

Begin your own dialog with the Lover of your soul and journal your very own whispers to and from His heart, even if it is only a few words. Remember, He is always whispering and He is waiting for you to listen to His heart. He has awesome words of love and instruction to convey to you today.

_____

_____

_____

_____

_____

_____

_____

_____

_____

_____

Dreams, Aspirations and New Wine

"Wherefore if any man is in Christ, he is a new creature: the old things are passed away; behold, they are become new" (2 Corinthians 5:17 ASV)

Your dreams are no secret to Me. Do not be ashamed to have big dreams. Am I not your BIG GOD? I am proud of you whenever you speak My words of wisdom. Oh, My beloved, you are coming to terms with life. You are becoming sure of yourself in Me.

I am happy with your newly acquired self-confidence. You are emerging, yet you remain humble and always rely on the graces from above. I will be very pleased if you remain docile and gentle. A gentle and quiet spirit I do not despise. I am a God of restoration, and I am restoring. Have faith.

The meek inherit the earth, and those who hunger and thirst after righteousness are satisfied (Matthew 5:6). Open your mouth and I will fill it with a new hunger beyond your highest longing (Psalms 81:10). The awakening of your heart makes it seem as if you could explode with the grandeur of it all. Yet, there is so much more.

You see, I take your old wine skin and make it new. You were made a new creature at salvation, and now I am regenerating what I have given you in order to hold more (2 Corinthians 5:17). New wine is coming, and you must be ready (Matthew 9:17).

Close your eyes for just a moment. Can you see Me? Can you hear Me? I am near. My breath is brushing across you. Embrace the moment. Embrace Me.

Waiting on a Whisper

Affirmation

Thank You for being so aware of my dreams. I will not be ashamed or fearful to dream big dreams. I could never dream bigger than You, therefore, my dreams could never be too big. Stretch me, expand me and oil me until my wine skin can hold all have You have planned for it to contain.

Yes, I feel Your breath on my face, in my hair, like a gentle breeze wafting through fields of grain. Blow through my life and let the grains of Your work in me grow, multiply and fill the lives of those who need it. You are my portion and I will be fruitful and multiply. Amen

Reflection

Are there any dreams God has placed in your heart which seem to big? Let Him resurrect them with the breath of His mouth.

Have you lacked in a hunger for righteousness, a hunger for Him? Tell Him. Ask Him for more hunger and take time daily, writing down what He speaks to you.

Chapter Two

Whisper Time

It's whisper time…Time to breathe Him in…Time to listen and reflect on what He has spoken to you and respond to the Waiting on a Whisper reflection questions or your own thoughts and insights. He is present…He is speaking your name… What is He saying?

Begin your own dialog with the Lover of your soul and journal your very own whispers to and from His heart, even if it is only a few words. Remember, He is always whispering and He is waiting for you to listen to His heart. He has awesome words of love and instruction to convey to you today.

_____

_____

_____

_____

_____

_____

_____

_____

_____

_____

Your Caring Heart

"For the whole Law is fulfilled in one word, in the statement, "YOU SHALL LOVE YOUR NEIGHBOR AS YOURSELF" (Galatians 5:14 NASB)

"So be merciful (sympathetic, tender, responsive, and compassionate) even as your Father is [all these]" (Luke 6:36 Amplified)

I love seeing your intense concern for the well-being of others (Galatians 5:14). Your compassion and generosity are the very reasons why I cannot and will not withhold My blessings.

I know you will be My channel of grace. I have made you to be so. If there is any contradiction to this in your life, choose to believe Me, not the circumstance. I trust in the covenant you made with Me to be a person dedicated to the well-being of others. In this, you fulfill the two commandments to love Me and your neighbor as yourself.

I read your thoughts, and I know you profoundly. I know your struggles to erase the dark spots of yesterday that endeavor to hinder your growth. Do not worry if there are challenges. This is the way of life. I was challenged and depended on every word proceeding from the Father (Matthew 4:4). So must you, depend on every word Holy Spirit speaks to you.

Chapter Two

Are we not walking together, journeying on the path we agreed to (Amos 3:3)? The path I chose before all time. I will walk with you all the way, never leaving or forsaking you. I will take you by My BIG HAND. I will be your shield against all enemies and your light in the dark, enabling you to encounter Me, to encounter My voice—the still small voice whispering to you the right words to say, the right way to go (Isaiah 30:21).

Yes, we encounter each other, and My hand leads you to the path we agreed for you to tread…I will always be with you, My beloved one. There is no other place I would rather be. All is restored in Me, regenerating what I have given you in order to hold more. You are a new creature (2 Corinthians 5:17). New wine is coming, and you must be ready. I am.

Waiting on a Whisper

Affirmation

My heart is overflowing with joy as I clearly hear Your voice. What more can I ask for? Your words are my heavenly guarantee all will be well. Your love for me confirms Your plans in and for my life. Prosperity in Your heavenly definition is in my house.

I give my anxieties to You as I trust in Your covenant with me. I will bless as I am blessed and You will meet all my needs while I go about Your business. I walk with You. I hold Your mighty right hand, for You and You alone are my shield and buckler. I depend on You. You will make me shine everywhere I go and in everything I do. You are blessing my family and all are restored by Your grace. All areas of our life have been restored in You. Thank You for the gift of restoration. Amen

Reflection

Seeing He knows your every thought and struggle, yet, loves you with a ravishing passion, tell Him everything no matter what it looks or sounds like. Receive His grace.

Reflect on the fact He is right beside you right now, walking with you each step your life takes.

Chapter Two

Whisper Time

It's whisper time…Time to breathe Him in…Time to listen and reflect on what He has spoken to you and respond to the Waiting on a Whisper reflection questions or your own thoughts and insights. He is present…He is speaking your name… What is He saying?

Begin your own dialog with the Lover of your soul and journal your very own whispers to and from His heart, even if it is only a few words. Remember, He is always whispering and He is waiting for you to listen to His heart. He has awesome words of love and instruction to convey to you today.

_____

_____

_____

_____

_____

_____

_____

_____

_____

Chapter Three

Walking With Jesus, the Good Shepherd

"that He would grant you, according to the riches of His glory, to be strengthened with might through His Spirit in the inner man, that Christ may dwell in your hearts through faith; that you, being rooted and grounded in love, may be able to comprehend with all the saints what is the width and length and depth and height—to know the love of Christ which passes knowledge; that you may be filled with all the fullness of God" (Ephesians 3:16-19 NKJV)

My beloved child, come. Yes, come and taste the clear waters of My unfailing love, and you will be refreshed. Forget the troubles of the world. Be drenched with My love now poured out (Romans 5:5).

In your silence and solitude, come into My presence. You can feel Me; you can even touch Me in your heart. I will rest in your being, and you will be in awe. Forget all your worldly cares. You will be transcendent as I come to rest in your weary mind. Many promises of the past, long forgotten, have been watered by your tears of repentance, causing them to grow within the soil of love occupying your heart. Be rooted and grounded in My love (Ephesians 3:17).

Draw deeply from the wells of salvation, and see My redemption come to fruition and bloom into fullness (Isaiah 12:3). The fullness of time has come.

Don't be so distracted by what has not happened yet, causing you to miss what is taking place right in front of you. In looking back, you lose. In looking ahead, you fear. In looking at Me in the midst of the here and now, you abound with faith and joy.

Only in the here and now can you be submersed in the moments of poured out love. All else causes you to be depleted, causes you to leak. The aroma of all your past burnt offerings and sacrifices are ascending to My throne, and I am sending refreshing help just in time from My sanctuary (Psalms 20).

I will dry your tears with gentle winds, and the passing of the singing birds will be a delight to cheer you up. When the wind blows, the branches sway, and the leaves sing melodies in tune with My eternal wind. I am there. The tiny pebbles you step on along the way will remind you of My abounding grace. Be not afraid! When the sun shines, beams of My secure love will melt your fears. When it is dark, worry not, for the moon and stars shine over you. And I, your Solitary Star, will be your light.

Yes, My love, be not afraid. You won't desire anything other than Me nor will you want for anything. I, like a good shepherd, in full watch over his sheep, will see to it that you will have more than enough. I am your Good Shepherd, and you shall not lack any good thing (Psalms 23:1-3).

Trust in My wisdom to know when you need a rest, to know when you need quiet waters. Follow Me always for I know how to walk on mountains, and I know how to walk through valleys (Habakkuk 3:19). I have hinds feet for high places, and I give them to you (2 Samuel 22:34; Psalms 18:33). The paths you're walking have already been traveled by Me. Fear not, worry not, doubt not, for I am able and willing. In fact, what you need and long for was already completed before you ever were.

Yes, the sun is shining, birds are singing, and tree branches are swaying. Notice how they do what comes natural without one thought or care. How much more are you than all of these? Don't ever think for even a split second that I get tired of telling you how much more valuable you are. I will say it till you believe what I say above all other things. You are My great LOVE. There is no other beside you. It is as simple as this: I adore you. Here now, let Me have that precious tear I see slipping down your face. It is precious to Me, and I have great plans to turn it into something else. Just you wait and see.

Your heart will become soft as I pour out My graces of unconditional love and forgiveness into its very depths. I am placing your heart upon My potter's wheel to mold and shape it (Isaiah 64:8). I want you to experience the warmth of My strong hands loving, holding, molding, and shaping the very fabric of your being. My hands of love wrap around you at this very moment, creating in you newness of life. Remember, I never stop creating. It is who I am, Creator.

As you forgive others and your own self, your heart will be cleansed of all defilement and guilt. My blood poured crimson red for this purpose and now you are dressed in white linen, full of love and bursting with joy. Though your sins were as scarlet, they are now white as snow (Isaiah 1:18). I will see to it there is no room for hate or vengeance, for My justice emancipates you from the tyranny you suffer at the hands of your enemies. Not one thought, plan, or scheme of the enemy has escaped My notice, and now it is time for him to pay. And pay dearly he will, with seven-fold justice (Proverbs 6:30-31).

Remember, the quickest way to justice is through the narrow gate of forgiveness. The sins of those you retain, are retained. The sins of those you forgive, are forgiven (John 20:23). Holding on to hurts disables you, My beloved vessel of honor. Let no little foxes of seemingly unimportant things seep into your vessel of forgiveness, thereby defiling the whole of it.

I will wipe away all guilt, doubt and stains of the past, making you as clean and fresh as a white sheet blowing in the soft breezes of a spring day. All your resentment, guilt and anger are wiped away. Forgive and it is forgiven. Do this even if you see no difference right away in the one you have forgiven. I did it before I ever saw any change in you. I loved you first. And you changed, didn't you? Be the first to love. Be like Me.

My job is to make you shine, to present you to the world as an image of who I am. I will see to it. You are shining. All your potential and the gifting once suppressed by a heavy yoke is coming into full bloom. Even now, you are blossoming in ways indiscernible to the eye. Some are indiscernible because you have a tendency to look at your failures and not your successes. This needs to change. Too much inward focus blinds the eye to see and causes an ungrateful, resentful heart. Be careful, My love.

Know in the depth of your heart how much I have already given you. I have given you so very much. These gifts, along with your abiding spirit, are to be used for the proclamation of My kingdom. I will not let you be hidden under a bushel. I cause your light to shine. I am the Solitary Star illuminating your heart and life. I shine through you and over you.

All I made you to be is never hidden from Me (Mark 4:22). Even if you can't see everything right now, doesn't mean it isn't there. I will guide you and will lead you to springs of refreshing water (Isaiah 49:10). I will send My angels to draw you near to people who will work in harmony with you, who will be in agreement with you, whose love will be pure as My love for you.

I love you so much, yes, so much, that I will not allow your gifts and beauty to be unappreciated or misused anymore. Take joy, for the birthing of your gifts is at hand. Let Me contend with those who hinder you (Psalms 35:1). I am putting a secret smile on your face, one radiating from your heart. Those who have held you back will wonder about your secret smile. Out of it, conviction will flow to others, and tranquility will reign in you like a peaceful river. Ingest My Word and let it nourish, and you will be at rest like a weaned child with its mother (Psalms 131:2).

Nothing you have ever shed tears for will be left unclean, unattended or forgotten. I have stored every tear away, every tear of longing, every tear of sorrow, yes, even every tear of unfulfilled hopes and dreams. I have saved every tear

(Psalms 56:8). I captured each one as it slid down your face. I hold all your tears in the cup of My hand, carefully placing them in My bowl of remembrance. They are the ingredients of sweet perfume, heady to My senses and precious to My heart.

I have in the past, and I am, in this very moment, transforming your tears into beautiful showers of grace. They feed a fountain of redemption like underground springs feed a stream. This fountain of grace and mercy—this fountain pouring forth sweet perfume, flows with grace to cascade over your life and heart. There is healing in your tears, healing of fractured and unloved places. Like the balm of Gilead, like honey from the Rock, like sweet anointing oil, they flow back over your life. A heart of humble forgiveness is a receptive vessel for this heavenly concoction formulated by My heart of enraptured love.

I am your Fountain of Redemption in all cases. I wash you right now with tears transformed by My infused presence and turned into an essence of healing love. My death on the Cross redeemed all. I came for you and for all you love. I am here for you and all things concerning you right now. Do you trust Me enough to let go? Do you trust Me enough to pour out your own fountain of transformed tears on those you love? You see, it isn't just for you.

I will always be near to you. Just call and I will be available because My love for you is infinite. As a matter of fact, I am already with you wherever you are before you call. I just love to hear you say My name, "Jesus."

Here now, come close; let Me collect the tears I see flowing from the underground springs of your heart. Be they from joy or from sorrow, I love them all. I love you. Your tears are now producing a time of joyful shouting (Psalms 126:5). Enjoy!

Prayer

The areas in my life once obscure are now becoming clear, as clear as the waters of a small brook, cascading its effervescence beauty across the rocks—cleansing the land. I look around and see the immensity of beauty displayed in Your many gifts of nature and my heart is in awe.

You have forgiven me of much, therefore; I choose to forgive first and to love first. Let not my eyes focus on things of this earth or be easily distracted by others around me. Even now my heart, ever so soft and pliable, is being molded by Your warm, loving, and capable hands.

I am safe with You. While I rest in You, the enemies of me and my family are contended with. We shall arise and shine together for Your Kingdom's sake. The enemy is even now returning seven-fold to me because of Your justice and my heart of repentance. I ask for and receive forgiveness and I give forgiveness as freely as it has been given to me.

I am standing under Your showers of grace. You have stored up every tear and are now pouring them over me as rivers of life-giving abundance. What the enemy meant for evil You have turned to good. The time of joyful shouting is here. Amen

Chapter Three

What is God Thinking?

Many, O Lord my God, are the wonderful works which You have done, and Your thoughts toward us; no one can compare with You! If I should declare and speak of them, they are too many to be numbered. (Psalm 40:5 Amplified)

Right now The Father is whispering your name and the thoughts of His heart are many, too many to count.

He wishes to reveal them like a landscape emerging from amidst the fog on a sunny day. Reflect on the tender whispers of love found in this letter. It is a time to love and be loved—a time to receive new gifts of grace. Pour your heart out to Him, the lover of your soul. Wait quietly and let the beauty of His love unfold before you as He speaks words of adoration and love.

Encourage yourself by writing down His words for they will give you new life in the days to come.

_____

_____

_____

_____

_____

_____

_____

_____

I Whisper Sweet Words of Love

"that He would grant you, according to the riches of His glory, to be strengthened with might through His Spirit in the inner man, that Christ may dwell in your hearts through faith; that you, being rooted and grounded in love, may be able to comprehend with all the saints what is the width and length and depth and height—to know the love of Christ which passes knowledge; that you may be filled with all the fullness of God" (Ephesians 3:16-19 NKJV)

"My beloved child, come. Yes, come and taste the clear waters of My unfailing love, and you will be refreshed. Forget the troubles of the world. Be drenched with My love now poured out (Romans 5:5).

In your silence and solitude, come into My presence. You can feel Me; you can even touch Me in your heart. I will rest in your being, and you will be in awe. Forget all your worldly cares. You will be transcendent as I come to rest in your weary mind. Many promises of the past, long forgotten, have been watered by your tears of repentance, causing them to grow within the soil of love occupying your heart. Be rooted and grounded in My love (Ephesians 3:17).

Draw deeply from the wells of salvation, and see My redemption come to fruition and bloom into fullness (Isaiah 12:3). The fullness of time has come. Don't be so distracted by what has not happened yet, causing you to miss what is taking place right in front of you. In looking back, you lose. In looking ahead, you fear. In looking at Me in the midst of the here and now, you abound with faith and joy.

Only in the here and now can you be submersed in the moments of poured out love. All else causes you to be depleted, causes you to leak. The aroma of all your past burnt offerings and sacrifices are ascending to My throne, and I am sending refreshing help just in time from My sanctuary (Psalms 20).

Waiting on a Whisper

Affirmation

I draw near to You sweet Jesus and taste the waters of Your unfailing love. You are faithful when I am faithless—strong when I am weary. All You are and have has been given to me. I rest my weary thoughts, my jubilant thoughts, and I sit at Your feet in a place of transcendent joy. There is no place I would rather be.

I root myself deep into the soil of Your heart and draw nourishment from Your great unquenchable love. Wash me anew with fresh fire and anointing.

I choose not to look back in regret, nor look forward in fear. Instead, today and in the days to come I choose to focus on You. Take my burnt offerings—my sacrifices and return them in the form of blessings upon those I love. Yes, help is here for me today, flowing from Your sanctuary. Amen

Reflection

What worldly cares and fears have distracted you from being in His presence?

In what ways have you been looking to the past with regret or the future with fear?

What is He speaking to you right now about any of the above?

Chapter Three

Whisper Time

It's whisper time…Time to breathe Him in…Time to listen and reflect on what He has spoken to you and respond to the Waiting on a Whisper reflection questions or your own thoughts and insights. He is present…He is speaking your name… What is He saying?

Begin your own dialog with the Lover of your soul and journal your very own whispers to and from His heart, even if it is only a few words. Remember, He is always whispering and He is waiting for you to listen to His heart. He has awesome words of love and instruction to convey to you today.

_____

_____

_____

_____

_____

_____

_____

_____

_____

_____

I Am Your Good Shepherd

"THE LORD is my Shepherd [to feed, guide, and shield me], I shall not lack. He makes me lie down in [fresh, tender] green pastures; He leads me beside the still and restful waters. He refreshes and restores my life (my self); He leads me in the paths of righteousness [uprightness and right standing with Him--not for my earning it, but] for His name's sake" (Psalms 23:1-3 Amplified)

I will dry your tears with gentle winds, and the passing of the singing birds will be a delight to cheer you up. When the wind blows, the branches sway, and the leaves sing melodies in tune with My eternal wind. I am there. The tiny pebbles you step on along the way will remind you of My abounding grace. Be not afraid! When the sun shines, beams of My secure love will melt your fears. When it is dark, worry not, for the moon and stars shine over you. And I, your Solitary Star, will be your light.

Yes, My love, be not afraid. You won't desire anything other than Me nor will you want for anything. I, like a good shepherd, in full watch over his sheep, will see to it that you will have more than enough. I am your Good Shepherd, and you shall not lack any good thing (Psalms 23:1-3).

Trust in My wisdom to know when you need a rest, to know when you need quiet waters. Follow Me always for I know how to walk on mountains, and

I know how to walk through valleys (Habakkuk 3:19). I have hinds feet for high places, and I give them to you (2 Samuel 22:34; Psalms 18:33). The paths you're walking have already been traveled by Me. Fear not, worry not, doubt not, for I am able and willing. In fact, what you need and long for was already completed before you ever were.

Yes, the sun is shining, birds are singing, and tree branches are swaying. Notice how they do what comes natural without one thought or care. How much more are you than all of these? Don't ever think for even a split second that I get tired of telling you how much more valuable you are.

I will say it till you believe what I say above all other things. You are My great LOVE. There is no other beside you. It is as simple as this: I adore you. Here now, let Me have that precious tear I see slipping down your face. It is precious to Me, and I have great plans to turn it into something else. Just you wait and see.

Waiting on a Whisper

Affirmation

You are my hiding place, my shelter from the storm, my Good Shepherd and I will not be afraid. All of nature declares Your beauty and love for me. Thank you for all the provision You have given and continue to give. I will not lack in any area of my life, physically, emotionally, financially, or spiritually.

You are my provision and I will follow You wherever the path leads. Without one care, I follow and my tears are collected by Your tender hand. I am walking in the *Light* with hind's feet on high places. Amen

Reflection

What areas of darkness in your life need an injection of His Light?

Reflect on the fact He has already walked the path He is now leading you on. How should this increase your faith?

Imagine your tears of joy and sorrow cupped in His hand, in His heart. Reflect on this amazing tender care He gives you.

Whisper Time

It's whisper time…Time to breathe Him in…Time to listen and reflect on what He has spoken to you and respond to the Waiting on a Whisper reflection questions or your own thoughts and insights. He is present…He is speaking your name… What is He saying?

Begin your own dialog with the Lover of your soul and journal your very own whispers to and from His heart, even if it is only a few words. Remember, He is always whispering and He is waiting for you to listen to His heart. He has awesome words of love and instruction to convey to you today.

Free Gifts of Forgiveness

"In Him we have redemption (deliverance and salvation) through His blood, the remission (forgiveness) of our offenses (shortcomings and trespasses), in accordance with the riches and the generosity of His gracious favor" (Ephesians 1:7 Amplified)

"So Jesus said to them again, "Peace be with you; as the Father has sent Me, I also send you." And when He had said this, He breathed on them and said to them, "Receive the Holy Spirit. If you forgive the sins of any, their sins have been forgiven them; if you retain the sins of any, they have been retained" (John 20: 21-23 NASB)

  Your heart will become soft as I pour out My graces of unconditional love and forgiveness into its very depths. I am placing your heart upon My potter's wheel to mold and shape it (Isaiah 64:8). I want you to experience the warmth of My strong hands loving, holding, molding, and shaping the very fabric of your being. My hands of love wrap around you at this very moment, creating in you newness of life. Remember, I never stop creating. It is who I am, Creator.

  As you forgive others and your own self, your heart will be cleansed of all defilement and guilt. My blood poured crimson red for this purpose and now you are dressed in white linen, full of love and bursting with joy. Though your sins were as scarlet, they are now white as snow (Isaiah 1:18). I will see to it there is no room for hate or vengeance, for My justice emancipates you from the tyranny you suffer at the hands of your enemies. Not one thought, plan, or scheme of the enemy has escaped My notice, and now it is time for him to pay. And pay dearly he will, with seven-fold justice (Proverbs 6:30-31).

Remember, the quickest way to justice is through the narrow gate of forgiveness. The sins of those you retain, are retained. The sins of those you forgive, are forgiven (John 20:23). Holding on to hurts disables you, My beloved vessel of honor. Let no little foxes of seemingly unimportant things seep into your vessel of forgiveness, thereby defiling the whole of it.

I will wipe away all guilt, doubt and stains of the past, making you as clean and fresh as a white sheet blowing in the soft breezes of a spring day. All your resentment, guilt and anger are wiped away. Forgive and it is forgiven. Do this even if you see no difference right away in the one you have forgiven. I did it before I ever saw any change in you. I loved you first. And you changed, didn't you? Be the first to love. Be like Me.

Waiting on a Whisper

Affirmation

My heart is soft and pliable in Your hands, washed by crimson blood. All my sins are white as snow, separated from me as far as east from west. You have risen up on my behalf and contended with my enemies. They melt like wax in a flame at the mention of Your name.

Every plan and scheme of the enemy is being revealed—they are being shouted from the mountain top through dreams and wise words. All darkness is fleeing and I am walking with a humble forgiving heart. I am forgiven and I forgive. I choose to forgive first and to love first for I have chosen most of all to be like You. Amen

Reflection

Take some time, real time, and let Holy Spirit show you any unforgiveness you are walking in toward yourself or another person. Remember, He loves you both the same.

What stops you from being the first to forgive, the first to love, or the first to repent? Break covenant with pride and self-preservation, forgive and receive.

Chapter Three

Whisper Time

It's whisper time…Time to breathe Him in…Time to listen and reflect on what He has spoken to you and respond to the Waiting on a Whisper reflection questions or your own thoughts and insights. He is present…He is speaking your name… What is He saying?

Begin your own dialog with the Lover of your soul and journal your very own whispers to and from His heart, even if it is only a few words. Remember, He is always whispering and He is waiting for you to listen to His heart. He has awesome words of love and instruction to convey to you today.

_____

_____

_____

_____

_____

_____

_____

_____

_____

_____

Bestowing Gifts of Grace

"Yet grace (God's unmerited favor) was given to each of us individually [not indiscriminately, but in different ways] in proportion to the measure of Christ's [rich and bounteous] gift. Therefore it is said, When He ascended on high, He led captivity captive [He led a train of vanquished foes] and He bestowed gifts on men" (Ephesians 4:7-8 Amplified)

My job is to make you shine, to present you to the world as an image of who I am. I will see to it. You are shining. All your potential and the gifting once suppressed by a heavy yoke is coming into full bloom. Even now, you are blossoming in ways indiscernible to the eye. Some are indiscernible because you have a tendency to look at your failures and not your successes. This needs to change. Too much inward focus blinds the eye to see and causes an ungrateful, resentful heart. Be careful, My love.

Know in the depth of your heart how much I have already given you. I have given you so very much. These gifts, along with your abiding spirit, are to be used for the proclamation of My kingdom. I will not let you be hidden under a bushel. I cause your light to shine. I am the Solitary Star illuminating your heart and life. I shine through you and over you.

All I made you to be is never hidden from Me (Mark 4:22). Even if you can't see everything right now, doesn't mean it isn't there. I will guide you and will lead you to springs of refreshing water (Isaiah 49:10). I will send My angels to draw you near to people who will work in harmony with you, who will be in agreement with you, whose love will be pure as My love for you.

I love you so much, yes, so much, that I will not allow your gifts and beauty to be unappreciated or misused anymore. Take joy, for the birthing of your gifts is at hand. Let Me contend with those who hinder you (Psalms 35:1). I am putting a secret smile on your face, one radiating from your heart. Those who have held you back will wonder about your secret smile. Out of it, conviction will flow to others, and tranquility will reign in you like a peaceful river. Ingest My Word and let it nourish, and you will be at rest like a weaned child with its mother (Psalms 131:2).

Waiting on a Whisper

Affirmation

Forgive me for concentrating on myself in negative ways, for always focusing on my failures and not on Your beauty in me. All that I am rests in You. I abide in You at all times. Even now the light You are in me is shining and will not be hidden. Angels are drawing near those You have chosen for me to work with.

Divine appointments are being arranged. The gifts placed in me are precious and ready to be used, not misused. You protect me always. I ingest the Word and I am nourished with strength and revelation to go, to walk in purpose and destiny. I rest in You and am never put to shame. Amen

Reflection

Have you valued the gifts placed in you as much as He has and does?

Has anyone ever misused or disparaged your gifting?

One by one forgive them and repent of any judgment against them for doing so and be amazed by the infilling you receive.

Chapter Three

Whisper Time

It's whisper time…Time to breathe Him in…Time to listen and reflect on what He has spoken to you and respond to the Waiting on a Whisper reflection questions or your own thoughts and insights. He is present…He is speaking your name… What is He saying?

Begin your own dialog with the Lover of your soul and journal your very own whispers to and from His heart, even if it is only a few words. Remember, He is always whispering and He is waiting for you to listen to His heart. He has awesome words of love and instruction to convey to you today.

_____

_____

_____

_____

_____

_____

_____

_____

_____

_____

Tears of Beauty and Enduring Grace

"You number and record my wanderings; put my tears into Your bottle--are they not in Your book?" (Psalm 56:8 Amplified)

Nothing you have ever shed tears for will be left unclean, unattended or forgotten. I have stored every tear away, every tear of longing, every tear of sorrow, yes, even every tear of unfulfilled hopes and dreams. I have saved every tear (Psalms 56:8). I captured each one as it slid down your face. I hold all your tears in the cup of My hand, carefully placing them in My bowl of remembrance. They are the ingredients of sweet perfume, heady to My senses and precious to My heart.

I have in the past, and I am, in this very moment, transforming your tears into beautiful showers of grace. They feed a fountain of redemption like underground springs feed a stream. This fountain of grace and mercy—this fountain pouring forth sweet perfume, flows with grace to cascade over your life and heart. There is healing in your tears, healing of fractured and unloved places. Like the balm of Gilead, like honey from the Rock, like sweet anointing oil, they flow back over your life. A heart of humble forgiveness is a receptive vessel for this heavenly concoction formulated by My heart of enraptured love.

I am your Fountain of Redemption in all cases. I wash you right now with tears transformed by My infused presence and turned into an essence of healing love. My death on the Cross redeemed all. I came for you and for all you love. I am here for you and all things concerning you right now. Do you trust Me enough to let go? Do you trust Me enough to pour out your own fountain of transformed tears on those you love? You see, it isn't just for you.

I will always be near to you. Just call and I will be available because My love for you is infinite. As a matter of fact, I am already with you wherever you are before you call. I just love to hear you say My name, "Jesus."

Here now, come close; let Me collect the tears I see flowing from the underground springs of your heart. Be they from joy or from sorrow, I love them all. I love you. Your tears are now producing a time of joyful shouting (Psalms 126:5). Enjoy.

Waiting on a Whisper

Affirmation

Every tear I have ever cried is precious to You, so precious they are collected and saved in a bottle of remembrance. As they slid down my cheeks, You cupped my face in Your hand, letting each one fall into a reservoir of reciprocal love. You have redeemed all things for me, including my tears. Grace and mercy are my constant companions—my dearest friends.

Faith and trust are my foundation and I will not fear. I let go. There is no safer place to be than in You. At the mere mention of Your name darkness flees. At the mere mention of Your name I am free. My tears have produced a time of joyful shouting. By faith I say, "I enjoy. I am restored. I am free." Amen

Reflection

Do you trust Him; have faith in Him to turn your tears in to joyful shouting?

In what areas do you need to experience the oil of heaven, the honey from the Rock?

Do you need to humble your heart in any way to become a receptive vessel?

Chapter Three

It's whisper time…Time to breathe Him in…Time to listen and reflect on what He has spoken to you and respond to the Waiting on a Whisper reflection questions or your own thoughts and insights. He is present…He is speaking your name… What is He saying?

Begin your own dialog with the Lover of your soul and journal your very own whispers to and from His heart, even if it is only a few words. Remember, He is always whispering and He is waiting for you to listen to His heart. He has awesome words of love and instruction to convey to you today.

_____

_____

_____

_____

_____

_____

_____

_____

_____

_____

Angels are Dancing

"The Lord your God is in the midst of you, a Mighty One, a Savior [Who saves]! He will rejoice over you with joy; He will rest [in silent satisfaction] and in His love He will be silent and make no mention [of past sins, or even recall them]; He will exult over you with singing" (Zephaniah 3:17 Amplified)

"For it is written, He will give His angels charge over you to guard and watch over you closely and carefully" (Luke 4:10 Amplified)

Beloved, apple of My eye, I am so very aware of your circumstances. I see the raging of generational assertions over your life and your family (Psalms 17:8). Just like I delivered Daniel from the lion's den, I am able to deliver you no matter what happens (Daniel 6:20). It is My desire and plan to do so. Right this moment, warring angels that I have sent are dancing a dance of war over you, a dance of deliverance from the onslaughts of the enemy.

I give My angels charge over you (Luke 4:10). Their garments are like flames of fire (Psalms 104:4; Hebrews 1:7). They emanate My passion for you. They dance over the child-like faith of your heart. They dance and sing over the promises I have spoken to you, and they will not return void. They dance a dance of jubilation over your newfound revelation of My love, a love which endures forever. Excitement in your heart shoots out rays and shafts of electric light, charging the atmosphere around you. If only you knew how I am drawn to every aspect, every essence of your life, your whole perspective would be different.

Therefore, I am opening your understanding to know how every word, thought, deed—even the tiniest inflection of your face directed toward Me—captures My complete attention. Paradigms and mindsets are shifting. I hide you under the shadow of My wings, and your atmosphere is now charged by the rushing of angels singing and dancing over you. Yes, I am also singing over you (Zephaniah 3:17).

Close your eyes and see. See Me and know I have always loved you. Before you were even formed, I knew you and loved you. I have a purpose and destiny for your whole family to fulfill. Embrace Me with faith. Look for Me to come, and victory will follow. Lay everything at My feet, all your expectations, desires, doubts and self-chastisement. I do not chastise you. I embrace you. Even now, angels swirl around you, dancing a dance of deliverance over your life. I need you, desire you for My purposes. I am jealous for you. You are Mine. All you have is Mine, and I will contend on your behalf.

Even though there have been winter days of life to endure, you have hoped in Me. Every season in your life can and will be infused by Me. No matter what, I inhabit the deepest places of your heart, and your thoughts always come back to Me. Your heart always hopes in Me.

Sometimes you forget who you are when you observe your own actions. I see things from a different perspective. I look at the true motive of your heart, and I am mindful of its wounds or lack of understanding (1 Samuel 16:7). A bruised and bended reed I do not break (Isaiah 42:3). No matter the depth of the struggle, be it measured in inches or fathoms, I care and I intervene.

Remember, hope in Me never disappoints. The circumstances of life produce a maturity in you as My love and faithfulness are poured out in your heart, bearing the fruit of hope (Romans 5:4-6). I have seen the sacrifice given to those around you—those you serve, those you love—and I am going to give honor where honor is due. I am honoring you for not growing weary in doing good (Galatians 6:9). I know sometimes you look at your own heart, seeing only shortcomings or focusing on the negative aspects of your attitudes and behavior. This is changing, for I have accelerated you into a whole new dimension of revelation and understanding. Today, wisdom is your portion, your bread. Today, you shift into a whole new level. Agree with Me and let it be.

Speak My name. Whisper My name. Close your eyes, and see your family, your concerns, held within the shelter of My name. Speak My name. Speak My name. There is power in the blood, power in My Name. Though you were far off, you are now brought near (Ephesians 2:12-13).

Angels, once only dancing, are now totally given over to the movement. So much so, they are intertwined in one purpose and become an intermingled force, creating light and fire. Light of revelation and fire are released to burn away all hindering foes, fire to cleanse to the very foundations of your life and family.

Holy Spirit descends, shrouds, and overshadows you in a cloak of peace and comfort (John 14:16). I, Your Comforter, have come to enclose you in the secret place within the wings of My heart, within the feathers of My comfort. Beloved one, once so fearful of Me, you are now enclosed in the beauty of My heart, radiating My glory.

Sweet dewy mists of My presence rise from around you, permeating the dry places of old religion with new revelation of who I really am. The Paraclete—the Holy Spirit, your comforter, teacher, friend and companion—is swirling freshness and freedom around you. He is dripping like the morning dew, and you are springing forth, My willing one, in the Day of My Power (Psalms 110:3).

I am your vision no matter what happens in life. Know this: I work all things together for your good (Romans 8:28). I do not leave you at the prey of the enemy. I contend. Envision Me standing before you. Let Me be your vision, your focus, and set your face like flint (Isaiah 50:7). See Me standing beside those you love, drawing and wooing with My Father's heart of love.

I am revealing to you and your family what a true Father is. Nothing escapes My notice, absolutely nothing. Look up to the mountain from whence your help comes (Psalms 121:1). Your help comes, not from any man, but only from Me, your Lord and Maker. Chosen one, look up and see how much I am engrossed in your life. Look up into My eyes of love, and know your time has come. The day of deliverance is drawing nigh for the completing of your family according to My order.

Be patient, and have faith (Psalms 40:1). Open your mouth, and let My faith pour into you, enabling you to endure. Open your mouth, and let My patient love speak through you (1 Corinthians 13:4).

As you behold Me with unveiled face, transformation born of My love for you is taking place. Transformation follows love. You are wonderfully altered by My love, and My love released through you transforms others. To love Me and to love them fulfills the highest call one could ever achieve. Everything flows from this principle. What a pleasure to use you as a manifestation of My love. Beloved, be patient; strengthen your heart, for I have come near to you (James 5:8).

It is not enough to have faith in Me. You must have My faith, and I will give it to you today if you open your mouth and speak the words I have put in your heart. Let My words fill your mouth. Imagine your heart like an open, beautiful vessel placed under an ever-pouring fountain on an extremely hot day. This is what I am doing for you: pouring My water, My faith, into the fiery circumstances of your heart. I am pouring My faith into your dreams and desires.

You see, at My right hand are pleasures forever more (Psalm 16:11). One of those pleasures is you, My love. Did you ever think of My Word this way? I imagine not. Beloved, You were and are the joy set before Me (Hebrews 12:1-3).

Acknowledgement of who you really are and the pleasure you bring to Me is not pride. It is necessary in order to walk in true identity, necessary to overcome the lies of the evil one. Know this: I have formed you with great intricacy. As you let go of all unprofitable things—all doubt and unbelief—you are cleansed, and I shape the clay of your heart into a vessel of honor ready for every good work. You are a good work. You are good (2 Timothy 2:21). You are a pleasure of My right hand.

I not only restore you, but I restore and prefect all concerning you (Psalms 138:8). I love your family; I love those you love, each and every one. I love you, and My kindness is leading all to repentance, and I wash you with My Word. Angels are dancing, Holy Spirit is descending, and faith is poured out. I am with you to do My good pleasure.

Arise and proclaim an end to all generational ties and bondage, for you have been translated from the kingdom of darkness into the Kingdom of Light. You are in Me, and I am in you. Close your eyes. Reach out and see Me, and see the atmosphere around you shift. All is complete in Me.

Prayer

Your angels dance over me. You sing over me. Hope swells in my heart like an open gate. Come in O' King of Glory and do as You will. I rest in You and Your plan for my life. All aspects of my life are delivered and restored to the purpose intended by Your loving sacrifice. Your blood saves me, covers me, delivers me and it redeems and frees me to be who You say I am—a pleasure of Your right hand. I settle into the comfort of Your protective, nurturing wings. Holy Spirit, I love You, need You and I respond with a heart of obedient praise.

Father, I give my all to You, my family, my hopes and dreams, yes, I give everything. I give my shortcomings—I give my prideful thoughts and I receive Your gift of righteousness and love. As I am being transformed by Your love, my love is transforming others as Your heart is manifest in me. I close my eyes. I see Your face. I hear Your song. Today is a day of angels dancing and paradigms shifting! The atmosphere is clear and I can see You, hear You, and feel You. Infuse me now and I will be changed. Amen

What is God Thinking?

Many, O Lord my God, are the wonderful works which You have done, and Your thoughts toward us; no one can compare with You! If I should declare and speak of them, they are too many to be numbered. (Psalm 40:5 Amplified)

Right now The Father is whispering your name and the thoughts of His heart are many, too many to count.

He wishes to release them and invade the places in need of the redeeming power of Christ's blood with the veracity and power of Christ's words, "It is finished!" Reflect on the blood of Jesus and the power of the Cross in relation to the needs of your life. Angelic activity is present to do His good pleasure. You are His good pleasure.

Ponder the meaning of being a pleasure of His right hand. Listen carefully. He is whispering.

_____

_____

_____

_____

_____

_____

_____

_____

Angel Dance

"The Lord your God is in the midst of you, a Mighty One, a Savior [Who saves]! He will rejoice over you with joy; He will rest [in silent satisfaction] and in His love He will be silent and make no mention [of past sins, or even recall them]; He will exult over you with singing" (Zephaniah 3:17 Amplified)

"For it is written, He will give His angels charge over you to guard and watch over you closely and carefully" (Luke 4:10 Amplified)

Beloved, apple of My eye, I am so very aware of your circumstances. I see the raging of generational assertions over your life and your family (Psalms 17:8). Just like I delivered Daniel from the lion's den, I am able to deliver you no matter what happens (Daniel 6:20). It is My desire and plan to do so. Right this moment, warring angels that I have sent are dancing a dance of war over you, a dance of deliverance from the onslaughts of the enemy.

I give My angels charge over you (Luke 4:10). Their garments are like flames of fire (Psalms 104:4; Hebrews 1:7). They emanate My passion for you. They dance over the child-like faith of your heart. They dance and sing over the promises I have spoken to you, and they will not return void. They dance a dance of jubilation over your newfound revelation of My love, a love which endures forever. Excitement in your heart shoots out rays and shafts of electric light, charging the atmosphere around you. If only you knew how I am drawn to every aspect, every essence of your life, your whole perspective would be different.

Therefore, I am opening your understanding to know how every word, thought, deed—even the tiniest inflection of your face directed toward Me—captures My complete attention. Paradigms and mindsets are shifting. I hide you under the shadow of My wings, and your atmosphere is now charged by the rushing of angels singing and dancing over you. Yes, I am also singing over you (Zephaniah 3:17).

Waiting on a Whisper

Affirmation

How I delight in You Lord as I contemplate being in the center of Your thoughts and heart…ah yes…the apple of Your eye. Every potion of my life and all the generations before and after are captured within Your vision. In one glimpse You see all. Thank You for delivering me from things I am unaware of, for showing me things I have no way of knowing.

I trust You to reveal all. Like David, I will adhere to You and Your word. I am faithful. Angels dance over me. My heart, my spirit is opened to understanding. I feel Your touch as You pull me into the shelter of Your wings. My mind is fixed on You and I hold the thoughts and intents of Your heart. I hear You singing Your song of enduring love. Amen

Reflection

Can you hear angels singing?

Hear Him singing over you. What is He singing?

Reflect on how even the tiniest inflection of your face or the most fleeting thought of love toward Him radiates from you and captures His attention.

Chapter Four

Whisper Time

It's whisper time…Time to breathe Him in…Time to listen and reflect on what He has spoken to you and respond to the Waiting on a Whisper reflection questions or your own thoughts and insights. He is present…He is speaking your name… What is He saying?

Begin your own dialog with the Lover of your soul and journal your very own whispers to and from His heart, even if it is only a few words. Remember, He is always whispering and He is waiting for you to listen to His heart. He has awesome words of love and instruction to convey to you today.

_____

_____

_____

_____

_____

_____

_____

_____

_____

Such Hope Never Disappoints

"…And endurance (fortitude) develops maturity of character (approved faith and tried integrity). And character [of this sort] produces [the habit of joyful and confident hope of eternal salvation. Such hope never disappoints or deludes or shames us, for God's love has been poured out in our hearts through the Holy Spirit Who has been given to us" (Romans 5:4-5 Amplified)

Close your eyes and see. See Me and know I have always loved you. Before you were even formed, I knew you and loved you. I have a purpose and destiny for your whole family to fulfill. Embrace Me with faith. Look for Me to come, and victory will follow. Lay everything at My feet, all your expectations, desires, doubts and self-chastisement. I do not chastise you. I embrace you. Even now, angels swirl around you, dancing a dance of deliverance over your life. I need you, desire you for My purposes. I am jealous for you. You are Mine. All you have is Mine, and I will contend on your behalf.

Even though there have been winter days of life to endure, you have hoped in Me. Every season in your life can and will be infused by Me. No matter what, I inhabit the deepest places of your heart, and your thoughts always come back to Me. Your heart always hopes in Me.

Sometimes you forget who you are when you observe your own actions. I see things from a different perspective. I look at the true motive of your heart, and I am mindful of its wounds or lack of understanding (1 Samuel 16:7). A bruised and bended reed I do not break (Isaiah 42:3). No matter the depth of the struggle, be it measured in inches or fathoms, I care and I intervene.

Remember, hope in Me never disappoints. The circumstances of life produce a maturity in you as My love and faithfulness are poured out in your heart, bearing the fruit of hope (Romans 5:4-6). I have seen the sacrifice given to those around you—those you serve, those you love—and I am going to give honor where honor is due.

I am honoring you for not growing weary in doing good (Galatians 6:9). I know sometimes you look at your own heart, seeing only shortcomings or focusing on the negative aspects of your attitudes and behavior. This is changing, for I have accelerated you into a whole new dimension of revelation and understanding. Today, wisdom is your portion, your bread. Today, you shift into a whole new level. Agree with Me and let it be.

Waiting on a Whisper

Affirmation

I lay everything at Your feet. I have held on to many things—held on to many ways of doing things on my own, leading to frustration and disappointment. I give up; I give in and join the dance of Heaven over my life. I trust. I believe. Shore up any weary places in me. Hope, love and faithfulness are poured out in my heart. I will not just hope in You. I am in You.

I open my heart, my life and receive Your hope. No longer will I focus on my shortcomings, for I can do all things as You strengthen me. I ask for wisdom and it is mine. Today I shift to a whole new level in You. It is done. Amen

Reflection

In what ways have you elevated your shortcomings and neglected to notice the true motive of your heart?

Even good things of the past can be a hindrance. What do you need to lay at His feet today, good, bad or indifferent?

Chapter Four

Whisper Time

It's whisper time…Time to breathe Him in…Time to listen and reflect on what He has spoken to you and respond to the Waiting on a Whisper reflection questions or your own thoughts and insights. He is present…He is speaking your name… What is He saying?

Begin your own dialog with the Lover of your soul and journal your very own whispers to and from His heart, even if it is only a few words. Remember, He is always whispering and He is waiting for you to listen to His heart. He has awesome words of love and instruction to convey to you today.

_____

_____

_____

_____

_____

_____

_____

_____

_____

_____

_____

Power in the Blood of Jesus

"...remember that you were at that time separate from Christ, excluded from the commonwealth of Israel, and strangers to the covenants of promise, having no hope and without God in the world. But now in Christ Jesus you who formerly were far off have been brought near by the blood of Christ" (Ephesians 2:12-13 NASB)

Speak My name. Whisper My name. Close your eyes, and see your family, your concerns, held within the shelter of My name. Speak My name. Speak My name. There is power in the blood, power in My Name. Though you were far off, you are now brought near (Ephesians 2:12-13).

Angels, once only dancing, are now totally given over to the movement. So much so, they are intertwined in one purpose and become an intermingled force, creating light and fire. Light of revelation and fire are released to burn away all hindering foes, fire to cleanse to the very foundations of your life and family.

Holy Spirit descends, shrouds, and overshadows you in a cloak of peace and comfort (John 14:16). I, Your Comforter, have come to enclose you in the secret place within the wings of My heart, within the feathers of My comfort. Beloved one, once so fearful of Me, you are now enclosed in the beauty of My heart, radiating My glory.

Chapter Four

Sweet dewy mists of My presence rise from around you, permeating the dry places of old religion with new revelation of who I really am. The Paraclete—the Holy Spirit, your comforter, teacher, friend and companion—is swirling freshness and freedom around you. He is dripping like the morning dew, and you are springing forth, My willing one, in the Day of My Power (Psalms 110:3).

Waiting on a Whisper

Affirmation

I speak Your name. Jesus, Jesus, Jesus, sweet Jesus, Your name is above all names. Your name is beautiful, tasting like honey on my lips. Your name is life to my very bones. Your shed blood brings me near, brings me within the very realms of Your presence—into untold dimensions of Your essence beyond the veil.

You enclose me; enfold me, wrapping wings of comfort and protection around me. Dewy smells of heaven penetrate me in this place with You. My heart softens and absorbs every word You speak to me. I am comforted, encouraged and infused. I am new in You. I spring forth with a willing heart. Today, my life and all it contains is given over to You. The sweet dew of heaven—the sweet oil of heaven drenches me and fills me today. Amen

Reflection

Holy Spirit is manifesting right now in a very special way, desiring to love on you right where you are. Listen carefully. It isn't just about giving. It is about receiving.

Let Him wash you, permeate you. Record what He says.

Chapter Four

Whisper Time

It's whisper time…Time to breathe Him in…Time to listen and reflect on what He has spoken to you and respond to the Waiting on a Whisper reflection questions or your own thoughts and insights. He is present…He is speaking your name… What is He saying?

Begin your own dialog with the Lover of your soul and journal your very own whispers to and from His heart, even if it is only a few words. Remember, He is always whispering and He is waiting for you to listen to His heart. He has awesome words of love and instruction to convey to you today.

_____

_____

_____

_____

_____

_____

_____

_____

_____

Transforming Love

"But we all, with unveiled face, beholding as in a mirror the glory of the Lord, are being transformed into the same image from glory to glory, just as from the Lord, the Spirit" (2 Corinthians 3:18 NASB)

I am your vision no matter what happens in life. Know this: I work all things together for your good (Romans 8:28). I do not leave you at the prey of the enemy. I contend. Envision Me standing before you. Let Me be your vision, your focus, and set your face like flint (Isaiah 50:7). See Me standing beside those you love, drawing and wooing with My Father's heart of love.

I am revealing to you and your family what a true Father is. Nothing escapes My notice, absolutely nothing. Look up to the mountain from whence your help comes (Psalms 121:1). Your help comes, not from any man, but only from Me, your Lord and Maker. Chosen one, look up and see how much I am engrossed in your life. Look up into My eyes of love, and know your time has come. The day of deliverance is drawing nigh for the completing of your family according to My order.

Be patient, and have faith (Psalms 40:1). Open your mouth, and let My faith pour into you, enabling you to endure. Open your mouth, and let My patient love speak through you (1 Corinthians 13:4).

Chapter Four

As you behold Me with unveiled face, transformation born of My love for you is taking place. Transformation follows love. You are wonderfully altered by My love, and My love released through you transforms others. To love Me and to love them fulfills the highest call one could ever achieve. Everything flows from this principle. What a pleasure to use you as a manifestation of My love. Beloved, be patient; strengthen your heart, for I have come near to you (James 5:8; James 4:8).

Waiting on a Whisper

Affirmation

You are my vision, my hope and the very breath of life breathing through my lungs, coursing through my veins. I trust You to work everything out in my life. I set my face, my thoughts and my love on You. I look into Your face, overwhelmed by what I see. I want to be as engrossed in You as You are in me. Change my heart—change my thinking as I meditate on Your Word.

Deliverance is my portion, my inheritance, born from Your nail pierced hands and feet. I open up to receive Your enduring faith, Your enduring love. I am transformed by Your love and others are transformed by my love. Infuse me with strength of heart for You are near, nigh unto my deepest—most hidden places. I give them all to You. You are here. Amen

Reflection

Take some quiet time and think on any wrong concepts of what a father is. These thoughts can be based on the actions of men in or out of your family. Release them out loud to Him.

Vocally receive the Father's heart for you and allow Him to release all His love, in the fullness of its transforming power. Do this daily, hourly or minute by minute until all doubt and unbelief are erased, till all the wrongful acts of men have been replaced with His truths.

Chapter Four

Whisper Time

It's whisper time…Time to breathe Him in…Time to listen and reflect on what He has spoken to you and respond to the Waiting on a Whisper reflection questions or your own thoughts and insights. He is present…He is speaking your name… What is He saying?

Begin your own dialog with the Lover of your soul and journal your very own whispers to and from His heart, even if it is only a few words. Remember, He is always whispering and He is waiting for you to listen to His heart. He has awesome words of love and instruction to convey to you today.

_____

_____

_____

_____

_____

_____

_____

_____

_____

_____

_____

You are a Pleasure of My Right Hand

"You will show me the path of life; in Your presence is fullness of joy, at Your right hand there are pleasures forevermore" (Psalms 16:11 Amplified)

It is not enough to have faith in Me. You must have My faith, and I will give it to you today if you open your mouth and speak the words I have put in your heart. Let My words fill your mouth. Imagine your heart like an open, beautiful vessel placed under an ever-pouring fountain on an extremely hot day. This is what I am doing for you: pouring My water, My faith, into the fiery circumstances of your heart. I am pouring My faith into your dreams and desires.

You see, at My right hand are pleasures forever more (Psalm 16:11). One of those pleasures is you, My love. Did you ever think of My Word this way? I imagine not. Beloved, You were and are the joy set before Me (Hebrews 12:1-3).

Acknowledgement of who you really are and the pleasure you bring to Me is not pride. It is necessary in order to walk in true identity, necessary to overcome the lies of the evil one. Know this: I have formed you with great intricacy. As you let go of all unprofitable things—all doubt and unbelief—you are cleansed, and I shape the clay of your heart into a vessel of honor ready for every good work. You are a good work. You are good (2 Timothy 2:21). You are a pleasure of My right hand.

I not only restore you, but I restore and prefect all concerning you (Psalms 138:8). I love your family; I love those you love, each and every one. I love you, and My kindness is leading all to repentance, and I wash you with My Word. Angels are dancing, Holy Spirit is descending, and faith is poured out. I am with you to do My good pleasure.

Arise and proclaim an end to all generational ties and bondage, for you have been translated from the kingdom of darkness into the Kingdom of Light. You are in Me, and I am in you. Close your eyes. Reach out and see Me, and see the atmosphere around you shift. All is complete in Me.

Waiting on a Whisper

Affirmation

I open my heart to Your faith, to Your love. I confess; I am a beautiful vessel of honor created for Your good pleasure. I am created to walk out a good work in the earth, to walk out an expression of You. O' what a wonder it is to be considered a pleasure of Your right hand. Your right hand upholds me, does valiantly on my behalf and holds an imprint of my name. There is no pride in this, only acceptance of who You say I am. I am enabled, encouraged and I stand to fulfill destiny and purpose.

Restoration and perfection of all things is here. I receive a restorative move of Holy Spirit in my life. I arise and proclaim to the past, the present and the future Your redemptive work. All ties and bondages of the past generations are being exposed and removed. My family is translated from darkness to light. Everything is shifting and what has not yet shifted will. Arise O' God, and my enemies are scattered. Amen

Reflection

Not only does He want to give you the pleasures at His right hand, He considers you one. Reflect on the immensity of this thought.

Something to ponder in light of the above. Since you are a pleasure of His right hand, that would mean you are also a gift to others around you. He offers you, His honorable vessel, and a pleasure to demonstrate His goodness, to others. Selah

Chapter Four

Whisper Time

It's whisper time…Time to breathe Him in…Time to listen and reflect on what He has spoken to you and respond to the Waiting on a Whisper reflection questions or your own thoughts and insights. He is present…He is speaking your name… What is He saying?

Begin your own dialog with the Lover of your soul and journal your very own whispers to and from His heart, even if it is only a few words. Remember, He is always whispering and He is waiting for you to listen to His heart. He has awesome words of love and instruction to convey to you today.

_____

_____

_____

_____

_____

_____

_____

_____

_____

_____

You are a Five Star General in My Kingdom

Then he said to them, "Go, eat of the fat, drink of the sweet, and send portions to him who has nothing prepared; for this day is holy to our Lord. Do not be grieved, for the joy of the LORD is your strength" (Nehemiah 8:10 NASB)

As you rose this morning I was present at your side, at the opening of your eyes. Angels attend Me, and their wings rustle as they stand over you, watching out for every aspect of your life and heart. Their wings stir the very fragrance of who I am and infiltrates the atmosphere of your home and family. Joy is arising from the very depths of your being and wants to be shouted forth in grateful praise.

Joy says to you this morning, "I am your strength. I am the joy of your salvation, so don't focus on your lack (Psalms 95:1; Psalms 118:15). Focus with a grateful heart on all the Lord has done in bygone days. Focus on the promises He has given you with a heart of faith. Feast on His acts of goodness, and look to the future with anticipation and desperation for more."

Satisfaction and desperation can live hand in hand, crowding out all attitudes of ungratefulness and lack. Live in the throes of divine tension and be amazed. It has not yet entered into your heart all I have planned for you, but it will (1 Corinthians 2:9). Like I said, "Live in divine tension, and prepare yourself to

You are a Five Star General in My Kingdom

be amazed."

Do not fret, My child. The enemy only has an inkling of the plans I have for you. He can only speculate about the people you are going to touch and bring to Me. The healing and restoration you give to the hearts of My people whom I send to you dismay him, and he does not want this to happen.

Therefore, he makes every attempt to stop you, for he knows you are a great part of ushering in My Kingdom in all of its fullness. There is going to be a last great revival, and you, My child, are a player in bringing this about. I have many of My children out there who are called by My Name, who are called of Me, but they have been greatly wounded. I want you to go to My bruised reeds.

I am using you to bring healing and restoration to them (Isaiah 61). I am using you to heal My wounded hearts so they can rise in the light of My glory and walk out their destiny. Yes, so they can take part in this revival, this new movement in the earth. Rise to the challenge, and know you are prepared in every way. Don't look back! A new day has dawned, and new revelation is raining into the very fabric of your life. Oh, the plans I have for you. They are truly amazing in every way.

I send people into your life who will love you through all things. They play a part in keeping you restored. They are an inner circle of people who will wipe your tears and laugh with you in triumph. They will hold your arms up in battle when you are weary. They will dance with you in your victories (Romans 12:15). They are your angels of mercy and support. Be mindful to do the same for them and others.

I do not want you to fear things going on about you. You are My Mighty Warrior. The enemy trembles when you lift up your hands, for he knows the calling and anointing I have placed upon you. Don't you worry about what others may be saying around you. Some of it is fear, and some of it is jealousy. Just keep your eyes on Me.

Beloved, you are a five star general in My army. I have chosen you to lead many in the Way. I have chosen you to receive plans and strategies to dismantle the enemy in this day. It is not complicated. If I only tell you to say one simple word of declaration, it will be enough, for the power of who I am is behind it and will vanquish your foes, My foes. One step at a time is all I ask of you. Listen and obey. Be wise as to good and evil (Romans 16:19; 1 Samuel 15:22).

Today I am promoting you. Come up higher in your own estimation of who I say you are. Come up higher and hear My heart for this generation, for the nations.

As you worship Me this morning, shutting out the world around you, I will come. Close your eyes, and enter into the Spirit. Enter in expecting Me to usher you into My presence. I arrived here before you, and I am waiting with excitement to meet you. Grab a pen and paper, for I am going to place some golden nuggets of truth in you today, some mustard seeds of incredible potential, eternal seeds destined to bear much fruit.

Remember the mustard seed, the smallest seed of all, and what it can grow into (Mark 4:30-32). If a natural seed can grow into such a marvelous thing, how much more will the eternal seeds from heaven grow in you? Sometimes you think your soil is bad, but I am here to tell you today, "The soil of your salvation is good soil and can grow anything. It is rooted in love, love flowing down from Calvary" (Ephesians 3:17).

There is no greater love, no more fertile ground, than soil saturated by My blood. When I give you a word of encouragement, a word of instruction, a word or prophecy, consciously place it in the good soil of salvation within your heart, your spirit. This assures growth. Nurture the Word I give you by speaking it, agreeing with it, and declaring it (Job 22:28).

Now take time to worship Me, listen and write down words I give you. They are the seeds of life that will bear much fruit today and in the days to come.

Arise from your place of worship this morning, and stand with the living creatures before My throne. Give glory and honor to My name (Revelation 4:9).

Let nothing distract or disturb you in this. Give Me the first fruits of your day today and every day (Deuteronomy 18:4). Amazing things will happen if you do.

Come to Me first with your problems, worries and concerns—before you ever whisper them to another soul. This is something you must train yourself in. Many times you hear the words of men, and they vary to such a large degree that confusion can grow. Come to Me first, and then let the witness of two or more confirm what I have deposited in your heart (Proverbs 15:22).

Arise from your place of worship today, and shout a shout of victory for your time has come. The more you praise, the more you confess what I have said to you, the more seeds planted in you will grow until they consume the very essence of your life.

Yes, I am standing with you, by you and in you today. Angels attend you in every way. Mercy and goodness follow you and overtake you in all you do (Psalms 23:6). Today is the best day of your life for it is a day I have made and planned for. Worship Me, and listen. I will tell you all the thoughts and intents of My heart for this day and every day after (1 Corinthians 2:16). Arise! Walk with Me for I am good and My love endures forever.

Prayer

As I rise this day, Father, I choose to revel in Your words of instruction and encouraging love. You are amazing in Your relentless pursuit of love. I stand in awe. Your joy permeates me to the depth of my being and I am changed. My heart is a habitation of good soil bought by Your precious blood. I am rooted and grounded in Your love and step up to the challenges offered to me. I will tend the seeds and the dreams You have planted in my heart, therefore; I will grow and many will find healing from their woundedness as I share the life planted in me.

I will come to You daily and give the first fruits of my life at the altar of Your mighty love. I rejoice in those sent to hold up my hands, to rejoice with me, to weep with me and I will draw from treasures planted in them. My heart holds Your thoughts, Your intents. I walk in Your plans which are ever revealing themselves as I focus on You. I rest in You, arise in You and walk in You today. Amen

What is God Thinking?

Many, O Lord my God, are the wonderful works which You have done, and Your thoughts toward us; no one can compare with You! If I should declare and speak of them, they are too many to be numbered. (Psalm 40:5 Amplified)

Right now The Father is whispering your name and the thoughts of His heart are many, too many to count.

The Lord wishes to shout them out like the Mighty Captain of the Host He is and enable you to stand up in the fray to be all He says you are. Imagine the Lord standing before the gates of your battle—before the gates of your need to overcome and receive a new revelation of identity and purpose.

What is He imparting to you and your mustard seed of faith? Arise and adorn yourself by verbal agreement with the words He whispers to your heart.

_____

_____

_____

_____

_____

_____

_____

_____

My Joy is Your Strength

Then he said to them, "Go, eat of the fat, drink of the sweet, and send portions to him who has nothing prepared; for this day is holy to our Lord. Do not be grieved, for the joy of the LORD is your strength" (Nehemiah 8:10 NASB)

As you rose this morning I was present at your side, at the opening of your eyes. Angels attend Me, and their wings rustle as they stand over you, watching out for every aspect of your life and heart. Their wings stir the very fragrance of who I am and infiltrates the atmosphere of your home and family. Joy is arising from the very depths of your being and wants to be shouted forth in grateful praise.

Joy says to you this morning, "I am your strength. I am the joy of your salvation, so don't focus on your lack (Psalms 95:1; Psalms 118:15). Focus with a grateful heart on all the Lord has done in bygone days. Focus on the promises He has given you with a heart of faith. Feast on His acts of goodness, and look to the future with anticipation and desperation for more."

Satisfaction and desperation can live hand in hand, crowding out all attitudes of ungratefulness and lack. Live in the throes of divine tension and be amazed.

It has not yet entered into your heart all I have planned for you, but it will (1 Corinthians 2:9). Like I said, "Live in divine tension, and prepare yourself to be amazed."

Waiting on a Whisper

Affirmation

I acknowledge Your presence and the host of heaven attending You who have come to do Your bidding in my life. I adjust my focus and set my face like flint in Your direction, according to the word spoken to me this day. I choose to remember all the good things You have done and are doing. I feed on Your acts of kindness with a heart of gratefulness while my heart cries out for more of You, more of Your presence. You are good and Your love toward me is never ending. Amen

Reflection

Have you been looking at things from a place of lack instead of having a heart of gratefulness?

Confess and readjust your focus.

What areas have you seen God move on your behalf and yet still desire so much more?

Start thanking Him and cry out for more.

Chapter Five

Whisper Time

It's whisper time…Time to breathe Him in…Time to listen and reflect on what He has spoken to you and respond to the Waiting on a Whisper reflection questions or your own thoughts and insights. He is present…He is speaking your name… What is He saying?

Begin your own dialog with the Lover of your soul and journal your very own whispers to and from His heart, even if it is only a few words. Remember, He is always whispering and He is waiting for you to listen to His heart. He has awesome words of love and instruction to convey to you today.

_____

_____

_____

_____

_____

_____

_____

_____

_____

_____

Instrument of Healing and Restoration

"The Spirit of the Lord GOD is upon me, Because the LORD has anointed me to bring good news to the afflicted; He has sent me to bind up the brokenhearted, to proclaim liberty to captives and freedom to prisoners; to proclaim the favorable year of the LORD and the day of vengeance of our God; to comfort all who mourn, to grant those who mourn in Zion, giving them a garland instead of ashes, the oil of gladness instead of mourning, the mantle of praise instead of a spirit of fainting, so they will be called oaks of righteousness, the planting of the LORD, that He may be glorified" (Isaiah 61:1-3 NASB)

Do not fret, My child. The enemy only has an inkling of the plans I have for you. He can only speculate about the people you are going to touch and bring to Me. The healing and restoration you give to the hearts of My people whom I send to you dismay him, and he does not want this to happen.

Therefore, he makes every attempt to stop you, for he knows you are a great part of ushering in My Kingdom in all of its fullness. There is going to be a last great revival, and you, My child, are a player in bringing this about. I have many of My children out there who are called by My Name, who are called of Me, but they have been greatly wounded. I want you to go to My bruised reeds.

I am using you to bring healing and restoration to them (Isaiah 61). I am using you to heal My wounded hearts so they can rise in the light of My glory and walk out their destiny. Yes, so they can take part in this revival, this new movement in the earth. Rise to the challenge, and know you are prepared in every way. Don't look back! A new day has dawned, and new revelation is raining into the very fabric of your life. Oh, the plans I have for you. They are truly amazing in every way.

Waiting on a Whisper

Affirmation

My enemy has tried to convince me of his prowess and deceive me by trying to make me believe he knows all Your plans. He tries to tell me I will fail. This is not so. He knows not the plans of Your heart for me. Since You are for me, who can be against me? Shall the created challenge the Creator? NO, he cannot!

You have chosen me to lose chains of bondage and heal the wounded through the power of grace. I am one who sets the captives free in the power of Your name. Even now the heavens are open above me and revelatory rain is falling into the recesses of my heart. I will not look back. I look ahead to Your amazing plans for me. I am Yours and You are mine. Amen

Reflection

In what ways have you been discouraged or worried about Gods plans for you or given into the enemies threats of incompetence and stopped short?

Confess your doubt and unbelief.

Accept His challenge for many are waiting to drink from the revelation He has rained and is raining down.

Chapter Five

Whisper Time

It's whisper time…Time to breathe Him in…Time to listen and reflect on what He has spoken to you and respond to the Waiting on a Whisper reflection questions or your own thoughts and insights. He is present…He is speaking your name… What is He saying?

Begin your own dialog with the Lover of your soul and journal your very own whispers to and from His heart, even if it is only a few words. Remember, He is always whispering and He is waiting for you to listen to His heart. He has awesome words of love and instruction to convey to you today.

_____

_____

_____

_____

_____

_____

_____

_____

_____

_____

Angels of Mercy and Support

Rejoice with those who rejoice, and weep with those who weep (Romans 12:15 NASB)

I send people into your life who will love you through all things. They play a part in keeping you restored. They are an inner circle of people who will wipe your tears and laugh with you in triumph. They will hold your arms up in battle when you are weary. They will dance with you in your victories (Romans 12:15). They are your angels of mercy and support. Be mindful to do the same for them and others.

I do not want you to fear things going on about you. You are My Mighty Warrior. The enemy trembles when you lift up your hands, for he knows the calling and anointing I have placed upon you. Don't you worry about what others may be saying around you. Some of it is fear, and some of it is jealousy. Just keep your eyes on Me.

Beloved, you are a five star general in My army. I have chosen you to lead many in the Way. I have chosen you to receive plans and strategies to dismantle the enemy in this day. It is not complicated. If I only tell you to say one simple word of declaration, it will be enough, for the power of who I am is behind it and will vanquish your foes, My foes. One step at a time is all I ask of you. Listen and obey. Be wise as to good and evil (Romans 16:19; 1 Samuel 15:22).

Chapter Five

Today I am promoting you. Come up higher in your own estimation of who I say you are. Come up higher and hear My heart for this generation, for the nations.

Waiting on a Whisper

Affirmation

Thank you for the people You have sent into my life. Please forgive me where I have taken them for granted in any way. Help me to be a blessing to them in all I say and do. I anticipate with gladness the new people You are sending. I refuse to listen to any grumblings or complaints against me as to the truth of who I am in You.

I choose to believe You and the Word You have spoken over my life. My eyes are on You, enabling me to come up higher. I lift up my hands in the very presence of Your throne and the enemy trembles today. He is disarmed when my eyes are on You. I come up higher today. Amen

Reflection

Acknowledge those in prayer that He has brought into your life.

Give praise and honor for all they have done. Thank Him for those to come.

Take time to lift up your hands in His presence as a statement of victory over the harassment of the enemy.

Spend some intimate time with Him and listen for His commands, then be obedient to do as He ask.

Chapter Five

Whisper Time

It's whisper time…Time to breathe Him in…Time to listen and reflect on what He has spoken to you and respond to the Waiting on a Whisper reflection questions or your own thoughts and insights. He is present…He is speaking your name… What is He saying?

Begin your own dialog with the Lover of your soul and journal your very own whispers to and from His heart, even if it is only a few words. Remember, He is always whispering and He is waiting for you to listen to His heart. He has awesome words of love and instruction to convey to you today.

_____

_____

_____

_____

_____

_____

_____

_____

_____

_____

Mustard Seed Faith

And He said, "How shall we picture the kingdom of God, or by what parable shall we present it?" It is like a mustard seed, which, when sown upon the soil, though it is smaller than all the seeds that are upon the soil, yet when it is sown, it grows up and becomes larger than all the garden plants and forms large branches; so that THE BIRDS OF THE AIR can NEST UNDER ITS SHADE." (Mark 4:30-32 NASB)

  As you worship Me this morning, shutting out the world around you, I will come. Close your eyes, and enter into the Spirit. Enter in expecting Me to usher you into My presence. I arrived here before you, and I am waiting with excitement to meet you. Grab a pen and paper, for I am going to place some golden nuggets of truth in you today, some mustard seeds of incredible potential, eternal seeds destined to bear much fruit.

  Remember the mustard seed, the smallest seed of all, and what it can grow into (Mark 4:30-32). If a natural seed can grow into such a marvelous thing, how much more will the eternal seeds from heaven grow in you? Sometimes you think your soil is bad, but I am here to tell you today, "The soil of your salvation is good soil and can grow anything. It is rooted in love, love flowing down from Calvary" (Ephesians 3:17).

There is no greater love, no more fertile ground, than soil saturated by My blood. When I give you a word of encouragement, a word of instruction, a word or prophecy, consciously place it in the good soil of salvation within your heart, your spirit. This assures growth. Nurture the Word I give you by speaking it, agreeing with it, and declaring it (Job 22:28).

Now take time to worship Me, listen and write down words I give you. They are the seeds of life that will bear much fruit today and in the days to come.

Waiting on a Whisper

Affirmation

Lord, You take even the smallest things and make something amazing, something eternal out of them. Forgive me for not giving honor to the small things You have given me. You are an amazing God. I will purposely acknowledge the seeds of life You speak to me and plant them in a deliberate way. I will nurture every seed of life like a mother nurtures a child in her womb.

I choose to put You in remembrance of all the words You have spoken over me. Today, I set my thoughts on You and my ears are attentive to Your voice. Speak and I will write. Speak and I will obey. Amen

Reflection

Spend some time in intimate worship and listen.

When He speaks no matter how big or small the word may seem, write it down.

Nurture the seed and be amazed.

Chapter Five

Whisper Time

It's whisper time…Time to breathe Him in…Time to listen and reflect on what He has spoken to you and respond to the Waiting on a Whisper reflection questions or your own thoughts and insights. He is present…He is speaking your name… What is He saying?

Begin your own dialog with the Lover of your soul and journal your very own whispers to and from His heart, even if it is only a few words. Remember, He is always whispering and He is waiting for you to listen to His heart. He has awesome words of love and instruction to convey to you today.

_____

_____

_____

_____

_____

_____

_____

_____

_____

_____

Arise and Praise Me for I Am Good

"You shall give Him the first fruits of your grain, your new wine, and your oil, and the first shearing of your sheep" (Deuteronomy 18:4 NASB)

"For who has known or understood the mind (the counsels and purposes) of the Lord so as to guide and instruct Him and give Him knowledge? But we have the mind of Christ (the Messiah) and do hold the thoughts (feelings and purposes) of His heart" (1 Corinthians 2:16 Amplified)

Arise from your place of worship this morning, and stand with the living creatures before My throne. Give glory and honor to My name (Revelation 4:9). Let nothing distract or disturb you in this. Give Me the first fruits of your day today and every day (Deuteronomy 18:4). Amazing things will happen if you do.

Come to Me first with your problems, worries and concerns—before you ever whisper them to another soul. This is something you must train yourself in. Many times you hear the words of men, and they vary to such a large degree that confusion can grow. Come to Me first, and then let the witness of two or more confirm what I have deposited in your heart (Proverbs 15:22).

Arise from your place of worship today, and shout a shout of victory for your time has come. The more you praise, the more you confess what I have said to you, the more seeds planted in you will grow until they consume the very essence of your life.

Yes, I am standing with you, by you and in you today. Angels attend you in every way. Mercy and goodness follow you and overtake you in all you do (Psalms 23:6). Today is the best day of your life for it is a day I have made and planned for. Worship Me, and listen. I will tell you all the thoughts and intents of My heart for this day and every day after (1 Corinthians 2:16). Arise! Walk with Me for I am good and My love endures forever.

Waiting on a Whisper

Affirmation

I come humbly before You today Lord to stand in Your presence with a heart of honor and praise. I give glory and honor to Your name. There is none like You. I give all my worries and trials to You in exchange for faith and peace. Forgive me for trusting others more than I trust You or Your Word.

I lean in to Your presence. I lean in to the thoughts and the intents of Your heart and they become clear. From this place of first fruit worship I arise to victory in Your name. All You have planted is growing as I stand before You with adoration and praise. My time has come and victory is assured. I confess, I shout, "My time has come!" Amen

Reflection

Is it your habit to pick up the phone or send an email about the happenings in your life before you go to Him?

Do you seek the advice of others first and then go to Him? If so, confess, repent and go to Him first. Give Him the first fruits of everything.

What seed, words or dreams are growing inside your heart? Reflect on any issues of doubt or unbelief towards them.

Offer them up with a heart of faith and listen.

Chapter Five

It's whisper time...Time to breathe Him in...Time to listen and reflect on what He has spoken to you and respond to the Waiting on a Whisper reflection questions or your own thoughts and insights. He is present...He is speaking your name... What is He saying?

Begin your own dialog with the Lover of your soul and journal your very own whispers to and from His heart, even if it is only a few words. Remember, He is always whispering and He is waiting for you to listen to His heart. He has awesome words of love and instruction to convey to you today.

_____

_____

_____

_____

_____

_____

_____

_____

_____

_____

Watered Garden of My Love

"And he shall be like a tree firmly planted [and tended] by the streams of water, ready to bring forth its fruit in its season; its leaf also shall not fade or wither; and everything he does shall prosper [and come to maturity]" (Psalms 1:3 Amplified)

"For he shall be like a tree planted by the waters that spreads out its roots by the river; and it shall not see and fear when heat comes; but its leaf shall be green. It shall not be anxious and full of care in the year of drought, nor shall it cease yielding fruit" (Jeremiah 17:8 Amplified)

You are the garden of My tender love. I am continuously watering and nurturing you. When your leaves wither and your roots go dry, My rain, yes My rain, will drench you. It will rain blessings, reminding you that I am a caring God. It will rain showers of deliverance, washing away any dust collected along the way. This must be so. I have important things for you to do.

The many surprises coming your way will remind you I am always by your side. You are anchored in My safe harbor. I am your sanctuary, your safe place.

I will see to it that you are well-watered, enabling you to grow robust and mighty as an oak tree. Your branches will be home for many searching ones as you grant to those who mourn in Zion consolation for their souls (Isaiah 61:3). Your discerning spirit will always lead you to aching hearts, and your patient ears will listen without reservation. This thing is already completed in Me, and now it is time for the fullness of it to reveal itself before your very eyes. Not only will you see and respond, you will see and hear My wisdom-filled answers and solutions. Be prepared to be astounded.

Yes, like the leaves of a mighty tree rooted by streams of living water, you will absorb the pains and sufferings of yearning souls, and in the process, you will exhale the exciting news of deliverance (Psalm 1:3). Like a parched land, your soil will eagerly absorb the rain, and it will flourish until the harvest is ready. All will be consumed into My hope of salvation as your life demonstrates itself as a living example.

The windows of opportunity outside the scope of your awareness until now will be triggered by your heart of adoring love for Me. The wildest and most impossible dreams you have ever imagined are coming to pass, unfolding blessings greater than your dreams could ever grasp. They are beyond the scope of all human understanding (Ephesians 3:16-21).

Have I not told you I do far over and above all you ask, think, infinitely beyond all your highest prayers, hope or dreams? I am taking the seed packed with potential, capable of holding within it a giant redwood, and nourishing it with all it needs to become an incredible monument of strength and beauty. Whatever you need to produce and grow, I have. Listen and discern My voice, and I will tell you all you need to know in order to grow.

I made you like a robust tree where people can find shade, shade of hope and a future in Me. The seed of destiny, the seed of My image is producing a magnificent, stately habitation for all around you. I have given you the richest measure of My divine presence, and today I say, "You are one wholly filled and flooded with Me!" Yes, My love, it is so (Ephesians 3:19).

Chapter Six

Your flowers will bloom in time, and spring will dominate your life. A life full of wholesome activities all geared towards the proclamation of My greatness will be your priority. Yes, this is to be your priority of supreme importance. You will call to Me, and you will heed My prompting with intimacy and absolute obedience. You will call to Me, and I will answer. I will give pressed down, shaken together and running over, for you ask according to My will for your life. When you ask according to My will, I hear you, and because I hear you, you have what you ask (1 John 5:14-15). This is so for you.

Your soft heart full of compassion and genuine care for others is very pleasing to My eyes. I can't help smiling at the very thought you have for the needy, the lonely, the broken. Yes, you love and long for restoration of all things in the lives of the downcast. This is My heart and yours as well (Isaiah 61).

Like a lightning flash, your quick mind thinks of ways to help anyone who needs it. You are My willing one, the expression of My serving heart. Unmindful of your own welfare, others come first. Yes, you are always last. Sometimes you don't see yourself as a servant, mainly because your idea of a servant differs a little bit from Mine. Anything you do for another is service, from the faintest smile to the greatest feat. Yes, it is a gifting I give all My sons and daughters, even though they may not see themselves that way. I see what you and all My kings and priest do. I have recorded every deed, and your account has accrued great interest. Draw on your account today. Your balance is great.

Your heart and My heart are entwined together. Like a three-stranded cord we are intertwined to form a rope of great saving strength and beauty. Yes, My heart celebrates the mere sight of you, comprehending how you will make it comfortable for others. I see the generosity in your heart, and I am exhilarated. How I love your big and generous heart. Your love for Me overflows, and you are ever willing to reach out to others. Indeed, our hearts, gushing and overflowing with love, are surely entwined.

I delight in the courage you have each time you get into a commitment far beyond your means. What courage you have! You are so much like Me, more than you know. Joshua has nothing on you, My Beloved. As I said to him I say to you, "Be of good courage!" (Joshua 1:9). Your excellent heart is full of courage and beautiful to Me. I am ravished for you (Song of Songs 4:9).

Because of your great courage, I am sending breakthrough angels to prepare the way. In your times of silent meditation, many Jericho walls of opposition will fall because your heart and mind are fixed on Me. I can't let you—won't let you, be harassed, burdened or attacked while you feast from My table with a heart of devoted adoration. If I could let this happen, I would not be who I am, your Lion of Judah.

Your faith that I will always make a way when there seems to be no way, does not surprise Me at all (Isaiah 43:15-17). Knowing how brave you are…wearing the helmet of a brave soldier always geared up for any danger…I cannot resist giving My ready help to assist you in any endeavor you plan. We are always partners. Your heart always believes beyond doubt. It never surprises Me, whenever you venture into anything pioneering. You are gifted with the courage of Esther!

Like Esther, you have been positioned for such a time as this. The day and hour has come for you, My beloved. I say to you, "Esther, oh, My Esther…" My Solitary Star, you will always shine bright because you bear My Light. Anywhere you go; your brightness will always be noticeable. Like a lamp, your brightness cannot be hidden. It may, at times, flicker in the beginning, but it will shine really bright to illumine dark spots in the lives of many. As I have illumined your darkness, you shall illumine others (Psalms 18:28). Be not silent, My Esther, in this day of your favor (Esther 4:14; Esther 5:3).

You will glow in the dark, and the truth of My divine light will guide you on your journey towards the work I have set for you to do since the beginning of all time—yes, even before the foundations of the world. You are meant to do as Esther did. You will gain favor from people of influence that will benefit a multitude of those in need. You will gain the favor from people in order to bless the Kingdom, and your influence shall be greater than you have ever known. Today, a trumpet is blowing, announcing the coming forth of your victory, unfolding purpose and great success.

I am commissioning you for a task only a brave and determined heart like yours can tackle. I am gearing you up for a very special task. I am assured of your readiness. In fact, I know it to be so for I have decreed it. After all, don't I know you and how you were made? Yes, I do, My loved one. It was such a pleasure to knit you, to form you, and now to launch you. Come, My Esther, and rise up on wings once hidden and fly. You have favor with God and man (Proverbs 3:4).

Along the way, there will be obstacles and entanglements posing as insurmountable foes. You will rise up like the eagle you are and no mountain will stop you. You will fly around some, fly over some, and speak to some. See and hear only what I am doing, and you will know which to do. They will not all require the same mode of attack. Some you will simply dismiss like swatting away an almost invisible, yet irritating gnat. Oil yourself in My presence, and those gnats will all flee. They hate the anointing and cannot stay in its presence. Like a good soldier, do not be entangled in things worthless, My love, and all is possible (2 Timothy 2:4).

You have already had some entanglements that seemingly have eaten up your precious time. The enemy has devoured what you have worked for in many past years, but like all great women and men of My house, you didn't give up. Now is the time to restore all things lost to you and cause a reaping to come forth.

I admire your tenacity to bear all hardships. You are My brave little one, brave like Esther. Yes, you are not moved nor discouraged. You are simply focused on Me. Your eyes are set before the throne of your loving Father, and nothing shall come between us, neither life nor death nor anything else up the enemy's sleeve. He knows he is a defeated foe (Colossians 2:15). Yes, he knows it. He is just banking on an increasingly failing hope that you don't know. You are coming to know this more and more. Because of this, it is harder and harder to catch you with any trick he might have. I will see to it you have the advantage of foresight, so listen carefully. I am the calm in the midst of your every problem. I am the joy permeating every day of your life. Receive all I have to offer.

Prayer

I decree and proclaim the Lord and the Lord alone knows the plans created for me, plans for prosperity and not disaster. The Lord is not silent and is revealing these things to me. You, Lord, are true to Your promises. You never change! You never lie! Your yes is yes and Your no to the enemy is just that, NO! I am the salt and light in the earth planted by You. My fingers are anointed and my heart plays the tunes of Your heart like a grand piano spreading sweetness and love to all.

My garden is tended by the Lord himself like a master gardener among beautiful roses and multicolored flowers of intricate beauty. He cultivates me. Others sent by the Lord, like robust trees of great faith, surround me to impart truth into my life.

Lord, You give me shade in the scorching heat of opposition. At Your right hand are pleasures forever more and You are sharing them with me this very day. I abide in You and You abide in me. As we journey together only Your will shall manifest. I am Your Joshua, Your Esther, Your shining star and You are my great love. I journey with You unafraid. Amen.

Chapter Six

What is God Thinking?

Many, O Lord my God, are the wonderful works which You have done, and Your thoughts toward us; no one can compare with You! If I should declare and speak of them, they are too many to be numbered. (Psalm 40:5 Amplified)

Right now The Father is whispering your name and the thoughts of His heart are many, too many to count.

He wishes to release them like a sweet fragrance stirred up by a soft breeze blowing through a flower garden on a spring day. Contemplate what it means to be a garden loved and cared for by the Master Gardener. What does He want to fill you with today?

What entanglements does He want you to separate from? Let Him tend your garden with words of love, encouragement and instruction. What is He thinking about you today?

_____
_____
_____
_____
_____
_____
_____
_____
_____

Garden of My Love

"And he shall be like a tree firmly planted [and tended] by the streams of water, ready to bring forth its fruit in its season; its leaf also shall not fade or wither; and everything he does shall prosper [and come to maturity]" (Psalms 1:3 NASB)

"For he shall be like a tree planted by the waters that spreads out its roots by the river; and it shall not see and fear when heat comes; but its leaf shall be green. It shall not be anxious and full of care in the year of drought, nor shall it cease yielding fruit." (Jeremiah 17:8 Amplified)

You are the garden of My tender love. I am continuously watering and nurturing you. When your leaves wither and your roots go dry, My rain, yes My rain, will drench you. It will rain blessings, reminding you that I am a caring God. It will rain showers of deliverance, washing away any dust collected along the way. This must be so. I have important things for you to do.

The many surprises coming your way will remind you I am always by your side. You are anchored in My safe harbor. I am your sanctuary, your safe place.

I will see to it that you are well-watered, enabling you to grow robust and mighty as an oak tree. Your branches will be home for many searching ones as you grant to those who mourn in Zion consolation for their souls (Isaiah 61:3). Your discerning spirit will always lead you to aching hearts, and your patient ears will listen without reservation. This thing is already completed in Me, and now it is time for the fullness of it to reveal itself before your very eyes. Not only will you see and respond, you will see and hear My wisdom-filled answers and solutions. Be prepared to be astounded.

Yes, like the leaves of a mighty tree rooted by streams of living water, you will absorb the pains and sufferings of yearning souls, and in the process, you will exhale the exciting news of deliverance (Psalm 1:3). Like a parched land, your soil will eagerly absorb the rain, and it will flourish until the harvest is ready. All will be consumed into My hope of salvation as your life demonstrates itself as a living example.

Waiting on a Whisper

Affirmation

I am the garden of Your great love and my heart beats for You Lord and You alone. You wash me with the Word and Your kindness leads me to repentance. Even now Your showers of blessing and deliverance are falling on me like sweet spring rain, preparing me for the task ahead. My heart leaps with excitement at the surprises ahead and like a child on his birthday; I will wait till the appointed time.

I will wait, but my heart will anticipate with great exhilaration the coming of My King and all He brings to me. Yes, I will wait without growing weary in doing good. Wisdom flows from Your throne and my heart is an open vessel, receptive to You. I go deep into the soil of Your heart and tap into the rivers of living water. I flourish in You. I am consumed by You. I prepare myself and say, "Astound me Lord for I am standing at attention before You." Amen

Reflection

Have you felt dry, in need of water from the throne?

Open up your heart in a time of worship and accept what He is already pouring out. Record all He says.

He has made you to walk in Isaiah 61. It always helps to give to others in the midst of struggle.

Who is He speaking to you about and what does He want you to step out and do?

Chapter Six

Whisper Time

It's whisper time…Time to breathe Him in…Time to listen and reflect on what He has spoken to you and respond to the Waiting on a Whisper reflection questions or your own thoughts and insights. He is present…He is speaking your name… What is He saying?

Begin your own dialog with the Lover of your soul and journal your very own whispers to and from His heart, even if it is only a few words. Remember, He is always whispering and He is waiting for you to listen to His heart. He has awesome words of love and instruction to convey to you today.

_____

_____

_____

_____

_____

_____

_____

_____

_____

_____

Heed My Call and Be Filled

"Now to Him Who, by (in consequence of) the [action of His] power that is at work within us, is able to [carry out His purpose and] do superabundantly, far over and above all that we [dare] ask or think [infinitely beyond our highest prayers, desires, thoughts, hopes, or dreams]" (Ephesians 3:20 Amplified)

The windows of opportunity outside the scope of your awareness until now will be triggered by your heart of adoring love for Me. The wildest and most impossible dreams you have ever imagined are coming to pass, unfolding blessings greater than your dreams could ever grasp. They are beyond the scope of all human understanding (Ephesians 3:16-21).

Have I not told you I do far over and above all you ask, think, infinitely beyond all your highest prayers, hope or dreams? I am taking the seed packed with potential, capable of holding within it a giant redwood, and nourishing it with all it needs to become an incredible monument of strength and beauty. Whatever you need to produce and grow, I have. Listen and discern My voice, and I will tell you all you need to know in order to grow.

I made you like a robust tree where people can find shade, shade of hope and a future in Me. The seed of destiny, the seed of My image is producing a magnificent, stately habitation for all around you. I have given you the richest measure of My divine presence, and today I say, "You are one wholly filled and flooded with Me!" Yes, My love, it is so (Ephesians 3:19).

Your flowers will bloom in time, and spring will dominate your life. A life full of wholesome activities all geared towards the proclamation of My greatness will be your priority. Yes, this is to be your priority of supreme importance. You will call to Me, and you will heed My prompting with intimacy and absolute obedience. You will call to Me, and I will answer. I will give pressed down, shaken together and running over, for you ask according to My will for your life. When you ask according to My will, I hear you, and because I hear you, you have what you ask (1 John 5:14-15). This is so for you.

Waiting on a Whisper

Affirmation

Lord, You are my mighty fortress and an all consuming God. There is none like You in all the earth or heavens above. My heart rejoices in the Lord God, maker of heaven, earth and all He contains.

The plans and purposes of God are now being revealed to me. I am becoming aware of all He has for me to fulfill. The seed of purpose and destiny are coming to fruitfulness in my life, producing towering structures of great strength and beauty.

All I need to grow is given to me by my nurturing Master Gardener. He is cultivating, tilling, pruning and filling my garden with extravagant beauty and great worth. I am full of the Lord's richest, divine measure of faith and image. My purpose is blooming and will bear forth the fruit chosen before all time. My heart hears and sees what my Father is doing and I ask and walk accordingly, therefore, I have what I ask. Today is that day. Amen

Reflection

Have you been afraid or limited in any way or stood afar off from God when it comes to asking for big things? What has stopped you? Write down what you have always been afraid to ask or lacked faith to believe for.

Put these request before the tender loving heart of the Father for He wants to give you your purpose and destiny, your desires and dreams. Let Him impart faith to say, "Yes and amen!"

Chapter Six

Whisper Time

It's whisper time…Time to breathe Him in…Time to listen and reflect on what He has spoken to you and respond to the Waiting on a Whisper reflection questions or your own thoughts and insights. He is present…He is speaking your name… What is He saying?

Begin your own dialog with the Lover of your soul and journal your very own whispers to and from His heart, even if it is only a few words. Remember, He is always whispering and He is waiting for you to listen to His heart. He has awesome words of love and instruction to convey to you today.

_____

_____

_____

_____

_____

_____

_____

_____

_____

_____

Three-Stranded Cord

"And though a man might prevail against him who is alone, two will withstand him. A threefold cord is not quickly broken." (Ecclesiastes 4:12 Amplified)

"And let us consider and give attentive, continuous care to watching over one another, studying how we may stir up (stimulate and incite) to love and helpful deeds and noble activities" (Hebrews 10:24 Amplified)

    Your soft heart full of compassion and genuine care for others is very pleasing to My eyes. I can't help smiling at the very thought you have for the needy, the lonely, the broken. Yes, you love and long for restoration of all things in the lives of the downcast. This is My heart and yours as well (Isaiah 61).

    Like a lightning flash, your quick mind thinks of ways to help anyone who needs it. You are My willing one, the expression of My serving heart. Unmindful of your own welfare, others come first. Yes, you are always last. Sometimes you don't see yourself as a servant, mainly because your idea of a servant differs a little bit from Mine.

    Anything you do for another is service, from the faintest smile to the greatest feat. Yes, it is a gifting I give all My sons and daughters, even though they may not see themselves that way. I see what you and all My kings and priest do. I have recorded every deed, and your account has accrued great interest. Draw on your account today. Your balance is great.

Your heart and My heart are entwined together. Like a three-stranded cord we are intertwined to form a rope of great saving strength and beauty. Yes, My heart celebrates the mere sight of you, comprehending how you will make it comfortable for others. I see the generosity in your heart, and I am exhilarated. How I love your big and generous heart. Your love for Me overflows, and you are ever willing to reach out to others. Indeed, our hearts, gushing and overflowing with love, are surely entwined.

Waiting on a Whisper

Affirmation

Lord, my heart is attuned to the needy, the downcast and the broken. Bruised reeds benefit from the wisdom and love placed in my heart. I have the heart of the Lord for the weak and unloved, for those dwelling among the highways and byways—those unloved by others.

I am quick to hear and quick to do all I hear the Father saying to me. Every act of service I engage in brings great benefit to those who receive from me and they are filled with life flowing from the river of His presence within me.

Humility, grace and mercy enthrone the deeds of my service to my King. I am a generous, big-hearted, expressive, devoted lover of the King. I am filled with the essence of my Father. Rivers overflowing with love pour through me. I am a three-stranded cord bound with a three-stranded cord. I am entwined with the Trinity for Their good pleasure. Amen

Reflection

The Lord has entwined His heart with yours, two three-stranded cords bound together by the cross. In light of this, what is He saying to you today about who you are and how He sees you?

He compares you to Isaiah 61. Can you accept this and His bragging about the beauty of your heart?

Reflect on this great love and service to others today.

Chapter Six

Whisper Time

It's whisper time...Time to breathe Him in...Time to listen and reflect on what He has spoken to you and respond to the Waiting on a Whisper reflection questions or your own thoughts and insights. He is present...He is speaking your name... What is He saying?

Begin your own dialog with the Lover of your soul and journal your very own whispers to and from His heart, even if it is only a few words. Remember, He is always whispering and He is waiting for you to listen to His heart. He has awesome words of love and instruction to convey to you today.

_____

_____

_____

_____

_____

_____

_____

_____

_____

Four

Courageous Heart, Brave Heart

"You have ravished my heart and given me courage, my sister, my [promised] bride; you have ravished my heart and given me courage with one look from your eyes, with one jewel of your necklace" (Song of Songs 4:9 Amplified)

"Have not I commanded you? Be strong, vigorous, and very courageous. Be not afraid, neither be dismayed, for the Lord your God is with you wherever you go." (Joshua 1:9 Amplified)

I delight in the courage you have each time you get into a commitment far beyond your means. What courage you have! You are so much like Me, more than you know. Joshua has nothing on you, My Beloved. As I said to him I say to you, "Be of good courage!" (Joshua 1:9). Your excellent heart is full of courage and beautiful to Me. I am ravished for you (Song of Songs 4:9).

Because of your great courage, I am sending breakthrough angels to prepare the way. In your times of silent meditation, many Jericho walls of opposition will fall because your heart and mind are fixed on Me. I can't let you—won't let you, be harassed, burdened or attacked while you feast from My table with a heart of devoted adoration. If I could let this happen, I would not be who I am, your Lion of Judah.

Your faith that I will always make a way when there seems to be no way, does not surprise Me at all (Isaiah 43:15-17). Knowing how brave you are…wearing the helmet of a brave soldier always geared up for any danger…I cannot resist giving My ready help to assist you in any endeavor you plan. We are always partners. Your heart always believes beyond doubt. It never surprises Me, whenever you venture into anything pioneering. You are gifted with the courage of Esther!

Waiting on a Whisper

Affirmation

Lord, I walk in great courage and my trust is in the You, whom shall I fear? My heart is ravished by you Lord and is full of grateful praise and adoration. Therefore, I do not fear as I embark on the path You have set before me. Every step I take is directed by You and I follow my path of destiny and purpose. Angels of breakthrough are making way for me according to the sovereign instruction You have given. I am saved from all my enemies for they melt like wax before the gaze of my

Beloved. Lion of Judah, You have risen up on my behalf and Your roar, like that of many waters, scatters my foes. I am not afraid. I am courageous, for You have gone before me to make a way where there is no way. I love You, my Way-Maker. You are the delight of my heart. I am a pioneer in the Kingdom of God with the courage of Esther, Joshua, Daniel and David. I am not dismayed. I overcome. Amen

Reflection

Has He called you to something intimidating, yet grand? Are there thoughts in your heart of great feats for the Lord left unspoken?

Today is the day to write them down and speak them.

He cannot resist giving you help today, so write down your unspoken desires, ask big and listen close.

Chapter Six

Whisper Time

It's whisper time…Time to breathe Him in…Time to listen and reflect on what He has spoken to you and respond to the Waiting on a Whisper reflection questions or your own thoughts and insights. He is present…He is speaking your name… What is He saying?

Begin your own dialog with the Lover of your soul and journal your very own whispers to and from His heart, even if it is only a few words. Remember, He is always whispering and He is waiting for you to listen to His heart. He has awesome words of love and instruction to convey to you today.

_____

_____

_____

_____

_____

_____

_____

_____

_____

The Favor of Esther

"So shall you find favor, good understanding, and high esteem in the sight [or judgment] of God and man." (Proverbs 3:4 Amplified)

"Then the king said to her, What will you have, Queen Esther? What is your request? It shall be given you, even to the half of the kingdom" (Esther 5:3 Amplified)

Like Esther, you have been positioned for such a time as this. The day and hour has come for you, My beloved. I say to you, "Esther, oh, My Esther..." My Solitary Star, you will always shine bright because you bear My Light. Anywhere you go; your brightness will always be noticeable.

Like a lamp, your brightness cannot be hidden. It may, at times, flicker in the beginning, but it will shine really bright to illumine dark spots in the lives of many. As I have illumined your darkness, you shall illumine others (Psalms 18:28). Be not silent, My Esther, in this day of your favor (Esther 4:14; Esther 5:3).

You will glow in the dark, and the truth of My divine light will guide you on your journey towards the work I have set for you to do since the beginning of all time—yes, even before the foundations of the world. You are meant to do as Esther did. You will gain favor from people of influence that will benefit a multitude of those in need. You will gain the favor from people in order to bless the Kingdom, and your influence shall be greater than you have ever known. Today, a trumpet is blowing, announcing the coming forth of your victory, unfolding purpose and great success.

I am commissioning you for a task only a brave and determined heart like yours can tackle. I am gearing you up for a very special task. I am assured of your readiness. In fact, I know it to be so for I have decreed it. After all, don't I know you and how you were made? Yes, I do, My loved one. It was such a pleasure to knit you, to form you, and now to launch you. Come, My Esther, and rise up on wings once hidden and fly. You have favor with God and man (Proverbs 3:4).

Waiting on a Whisper

Affirmation

Lord, I have been positioned in this hour, this day, and this time for a specific purpose designed by the Father for me and me alone. I will not miss it. I am obedient and willing to do whatever the Father asks of me without delay or concern for my own well being. I am a bearer of Your light Lord. I am salt in the earth. The light of Your presence illumines my darkness and the darkness of those around me.

Favor and blessings are my portions and they are plentiful in my life, enabling me to be a blessing to all I come in contact with. Blessing and favor with God and man is my portion, my daily bread, served to me at the banqueting table of my Beloved. I am fashioned and formed—specifically knit—to be a beautiful garment to bless and cover others. Commissioned by the Lord, my hidden wings of purpose are unfolding and I rise up like an eagle to fly. I soar over, around and through mountains according to the instruction of the Lord which I hear clearly. I arise and fly. Amen

Reflection

Have you lacked favor in any area of your life? He has purchased your life at great cost. Why would He stop now? There is no way for Him to do this, to stop that is. Come to Him with this understanding and receive your place in history and the favor to carry out such a time as this.

Stand before Him in a posture of receiving and let Him adorn you with great courage; let Him press great courage into the depths of your being. Listen carefully to what He says and agree. Please agree. It is imperative to success in the days ahead.

Chapter Six

Whisper Time

It's whisper time…Time to breathe Him in…Time to listen and reflect on what He has spoken to you and respond to the Waiting on a Whisper reflection questions or your own thoughts and insights. He is present…He is speaking your name… What is He saying?

Begin your own dialog with the Lover of your soul and journal your very own whispers to and from His heart, even if it is only a few words. Remember, He is always whispering and He is waiting for you to listen to His heart. He has awesome words of love and instruction to convey to you today.

Six

Disengage from Any Entanglement

"No soldier when in service gets entangled in the enterprises of [civilian] life; his aim is to satisfy and please the one who enlisted him." (2 Timothy 2:4 Amplified)

"[God] disarmed the principalities and powers that were ranged against us and made a bold display and public example of them, in triumphing over them in Him and in it [the cross]." (Colossians 2:15 Amplified)

Along the way, there will be obstacles and entanglements posing as insurmountable foes. You will rise up like the eagle you are and no mountain will stop you. You will fly around some, fly over some, and speak to some. See and hear only what I am doing, and you will know which to do. They will not all require the same mode of attack. Some you will simply dismiss like swatting away an almost invisible, yet irritating gnat.

Oil yourself in My presence, and those gnats will all flee. They hate the anointing and cannot stay in its presence. Like a good soldier, do not be entangled in things worthless, My love, and all is possible (2 Timothy 2:4).

You have already had some entanglements that seemingly have eaten up your precious time. The enemy has devoured what you have worked for in many past years, but like all great women and men of My house, you didn't give up. Now is the time to restore all things lost to you and cause a reaping to come forth.

I admire your tenacity to bear all hardships. You are My brave little one, brave like Esther. Yes, you are not moved nor discouraged. You are simply focused on Me. Your eyes are set before the throne of your loving Father, and nothing shall come between us, neither life nor death nor anything else up the enemy's sleeve. He knows he is a defeated foe (Colossians 2:15). Yes, he knows it. He is just banking on an increasingly failing hope that you don't know. You are coming to know this more and more.

Because of this, it is harder and harder to catch you with any trick he might have. I will see to it you have the advantage of foresight, so listen carefully. I am the calm in the midst of your every problem. I am the joy permeating every day of your life. Reccive all I have to offer.

Waiting on a Whisper

Affirmation

Lord, all obstacles and entanglements sent by the enemy or those created by the desires of my own flesh must now submit to You as I resist the evil one and all his devices, schemes and lies. I rise and fly. I drip in the oil of Your presence and anointing flows from my obedient and humble heart. All pride flees at the mention of Your name and sufferings. Gnats of irritation and frustration do not come nigh me in this secret place of intimate habitation. The entanglements and opposition of the past robbed from me, but You have come and given me life and life more abundantly (John 10:10).

All is restored seven-fold and nothing will be held back or at bay. I have a tenacious, persevering heart. I am a brave heart. I discern the schemes and tricks the enemy tries to hide up his sleeve for I have the Spirit of the Lord operating within me. Holy Spirit reveals hidden things to me and I am walking in heavenly foresight. The joy of the Lord is my strength. He is with me. Amen

Reflection

The time has come to untangle yourself and if you do not know how, Holy Spirit will show you. What entanglements or distractions have you encountered lately? Make a decision of obedience and be freed by the hand of Father.

His Word says nothing will come between you and the love of your Father in Heaven. In light of this He has a vested interest in accomplishing your deliverance and victory enabling His plans for you to come about. Think on this very carefully and record your entanglements and wait for the wisdom from Him to be set free.

Chapter Six

Whisper Time

It's whisper time…Time to breathe Him in…Time to listen and reflect on what He has spoken to you and respond to the Waiting on a Whisper reflection questions or your own thoughts and insights. He is present…He is speaking your name… What is He saying?

Begin your own dialog with the Lover of your soul and journal your very own whispers to and from His heart, even if it is only a few words. Remember, He is always whispering and He is waiting for you to listen to His heart. He has awesome words of love and instruction to convey to you today.

_____

_____

_____

_____

_____

_____

_____

_____

_____

_____

Introducing Brenda Craig — Friend and extravagant worshipper of God. Brenda has served the Lord with Duane, her husband of 32 years, since 1980. Alongside her husband, she has taught "Two Becoming One" marriage class, served as Ministry Coordinator, Intercessory Prayer Coordinator, Prophetic Ministry Coordinator, Home Group Leader and Prayer Leader for Prophetic Prayer Ministry, conducted personal ministry and counseling. Together with her husband, she has served in many leadership roles within the local church and currently serves with her husband on the Wider Council at River City House of Prayer in San Antonio, TX under the guidance and counsel of Pastors William and Angela Nunez.

Brenda is a graduate of the International Prophetic Mentoring Counsel. She has had many years of training through various ministries such as: Dr. Bill Hamon, Patricia King's Glory School, Mary Lindow, Kansas City IHOP, Apostle John Dean of Alliance International Ministries and many others.

You can read more of Brenda's writings at *www.allaboutprayer.org* under *Hearing God* and at *www.faithwriters.com* where she garnered 1st place for her poem "Surrendered to Red" which has been published in Faith Writers *Abundance of Life*.

Brenda founded *Journals of the Heart* in 2006 after spending three years on the backside of the desert where she recorded some seventy love letters whispered from the Father's heart. Convinced others could glean from her journey and in response to a prophetic dream where she was lead to *www.allaboutgod.com,* she began *www.journalsoftheheart.com. Journals of the Heart* is a place of prophetic revelation, insight and mentoring to those in need.

During the short time since its inception Father has seen fit to add to Brenda's team by sending Eustacia Siman Martinez and Veryl Williams to be mentored and they now contribute to the dream in Brenda's heart. They provided inspiration for several of the whispers included in, *Carvings In His Palm, What God Thinks When He Whispers Your Name*.

Brenda is currently conducting classes on *Soaking with a Purpose*, teaching others how to hear and journal the heart of God, using what Holy Spirit gives them as decrees over their life, according to Job 22:28. Out of this passion she has also developed *www.soakingwithapurpose.com* and *www.spiritualdecrees.com*. Her dream—her desire is to see the lives of believers transformed into an intimate pursuit of God through the power of communion and declaration. Brenda resides in San Antonio, TX with her husband Duane, son Daniel and delightful Shi Tzu, Ellie Mae.

Resources

I pray the following resources will be of great benefit in your life. I have included those who have made a relational and spiritual difference in my life. Be sure and check out their websites and you will be as blessed as I have been.

Randall Niles of (www.allaboutgod.com and www.allaboutprayer.org)
Randall and his team have been amazing to work with and All About God is a tremendous educational resource to the body of Christ and the world.

Candace House of (www.candacehouse.org)
Candace is the founder of Ruach Chayah (Breath of Life) Global Ministries. Check out her life changing book, *Shut The Door, "It Is Well"*

Raquel Soto of (www.acts1614.org)
Raquel Soto, author of *The 1 Minute Guide to Health, Wealth, and Happiness, Wisdom from the book of Proverbs*, captures the thoughts of God's heart and translates them into relevant truth.

Vince and Becky Perna of (www.riveroflifecbs.com)
River of Life is a family-owned and operated full service Christian bookstore. The Pernas have owned River of Life since 1990. Be sure and check out all their music and great books.

Joe and Susan Vigliano of (www.focus-on-prayer.com)
Joe authored *The 11 Day Path--Overcoming Stumbling Blocks to Belief.*

Tiffany Ann Lewis of (www.tiffanyannlewis.com)
Tiffany Ann is a prophetic minstrel, psalmist, and speaker. I know you will enjoy her music and be encouraged by her great heart and passionate love for Christ.

To Order Copies of Titles by Brenda Craig

1. **Call (210) 663-5069;**

2. **Order online: www.journalsoftheheart.com; or**

3. **Fill out this Form and FAX (830- 438-3189) or Mail to:**

   Spirit Food for Life Publishing
   P.O. Box 5271
   San Antonio, TX, 78201

Name _____
Address _____
Address _____
City _____ State _____ Zip _____

Payment method (circle one)   check   money order

E-mail address _____

Phone _____

Quanity:

_____   Carvings in His Palm

Quanity of Books ____ X $12.95 ea. $ _____
Shipping* $ _____
Tax ** $ _____

Shipment Total $ _____

*Shipping: (1) Book $5.00   Additional Books: $1.00 each
Contact for International shipping cost

**Taxes: Texas residents, add 8.25% sales tax.
(Call for discounts on bulk orders for churches, ministries and resellers.)